strategize!
experiential exercises in
strategic management

Julie Siciliano

Western New England College

C. Gopinath

Suffolk University

SOUTH-WESTERN

™

THOMSON LEARNING

Australia · Canada · Mexico · Singapore · Spain · United Kingdom · United States

Strategize! Experiential Exercises in Strategic Management, 1e by Julie I. Siciliano & C. Gopinath

VICE PRESIDENT/PUBLISHER:	Jack W. Calhoun
EXECUTIVE EDITOR:	John Szilagyi
MARKETING MANAGER:	Rob Bloom
DEVELOPMENTAL EDITOR:	Judith O'Neill
PRODUCTION EDITOR:	Elizabeth A. Shipp
MEDIA TECHNOLOGY EDITOR:	Vicky True
MEDIA DEVELOPMENTAL EDITOR:	Kristen Meere
MEDIA PRODUCTION EDITOR:	Mark Sears
MANUFACTURING COORDINATOR:	Sandee Milewski
EDITORIAL PRODUCTION AND INTERNAL DESIGN:	James Reidel, LogaTorial Editorial Services
COVER DESIGN:	Rick Moore
COVER IMAGE:	Photo Disc, Inc.
PRINTER:	Globus Printing, Inc.

Printed in the United States of America
1 2 3 4 5 04 03 02 01

For more information contact South-Western, 5101 Madison Road, Cincinnati, Ohio, 45227 or find us on the Internet at http://www.swcollege.com.

For permission to use material from this text or product, contact us by
• telephone: 1-800-730-2214
• fax: 1-800-730-2215
• web: http://www.thomsonrights.com

ISBN: 0-324-06653-8

Introduction

T he strategic management/business policy course is among the most challenging in the business curriculum—and for good reason. It is designed to teach the skills of strategic thinking and analysis, and it requires that students integrate information from courses throughout the business curriculum. The goal of the course is equally challenging: to learn strategic management theories and concepts in order to "do" strategy.

Cases have been an important and traditional component of the strategic management course. Indeed, cases are excellent devices for compelling students to appreciate the intricacies of making decisions within a context. However, what is often missing in case-driven courses is that critical bridge between understanding strategic models and applying them in ways that ensure active engagement with case material at levels beyond the merely factual. Computer-based strategy simulations, likewise, give students lots of practice in making decisions, but they are also somewhat limiting as students rarely get to experiment with appropriate models or concepts before attempting to apply them to simulation specifics. *Strategize!* bridges this gap by providing a series of "Strategy Sessions" through which students can evaluate theories in incremental and structured ways in advance of applying them to resolve strategic business problems.

These 17 unique action-oriented Strategy Sessions present experiential exercises and projects for use in class and out: as breaks away from straight lectures, as segues to case discussions, as homework, as collaborative assignments, as lecture launchers, as preclass case preparation, and similar alternatives. Exercises can be drawn on when theories are first introduced and discussed in class or at other times during the semester to reinforce previously reviewed material.

Each Strategy Session makes a complete turn through the active learning cycle of thought, action, feedback, and assessment. In our view, working productively, staying motivated, and actively exploring potentially relevant theories generate a greater probability of successfully achieving the goals of demanding capstone courses, such as strategic management, and so we have incorporated these aims into our exercises. Figure I.1 depicts the experiential learning cycle, as we implement it.

Our approach to experiential learning, as Figure I.1 shows, incorporates successive rounds of reflection, experimentation, and assessment. Our exercises focus on building abilities to apply appropriate strategic theories and models to reach meaningful conclusions, along the way strengthening critical thinking skills, analytical skills, and the ability to make defensible decisions and generate persuasive arguments.

Testing the strengths and limitations of theories and getting regular feedback about one's understanding of them form an important complement to the case-study method. The design of each Strategy Session brings together a number of elements that supports the thinking/acting/assessing components of the active learning cycle:

1. Brief explanations—or readings—of relevant concepts, wherein the academic purpose of the exercise is made absolutely clear.
2. Structured applications.
3. Instructor-facilitated debriefings.
4. Assessments of individual participation and accountability.
5. Assessments of overall learning.

Figure I.1   Experiential Learning Cycle

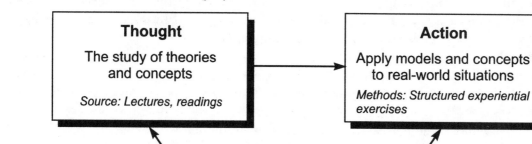

Some Strategy Sessions require teams, whereas others may be completed on an individual or team basis, depending on instructor preference. To promote individual accountability, many sessions have assessment forms to document the student's understanding of the work before delving into an activity. All sessions have assessments to be administered after each exercise. The forms vary and either size up how well students fit strategic concepts and tools to given problems or provide feedback to the instructor about the class session in general. (Assessment literature suggests that the formats vary from one session to another.)

As in any course that revolves around experiential methods, the instructor plays a crucial role acting as moderator, questioner, and lecturer, probing for details, for support for arguments, and for alternative courses of action. *Strategize!*, through the simultaneous publication of a resource manual for instructors, can provide useful strategies for managing exercises in the classroom. More information about instructor support materials is available at **http://siciliano.swcollege. com**—but a quick reference of Figure I.2, the Strategy Session Matrix, shows how each Strategy Session complements chapter discussions in several leading strategic management texts. Detailed guidelines for providing feedback and assessing student learning are provided in the aforementioned instructor's manual (ISBN 0-324-07189-2).

Organization of the Book

Strategize! is divided into five parts. Parts I, II, and III, on understanding strategic management, designing strategy, and implementing strategy, set up a series of Strategy Sessions designed primarily for in-class use. The sequencing of Strategy Sessions is key as it mimics the steps in the strategic management process common to most textbooks in the field. Strategy Sessions are intended to provide students with an active experience of concepts. Each session opens with a precisely stated learning objective, followed by a short reading that frames the theory or concept that is highlighted in the real drama: the session's featured exercise. As noted earlier, exercises have been developed for students to complete individually or in groups. However, we have also designed them to increase variety and interest in the classroom.

Part IV features an industry analysis of the mature lodging industry and the rapidly changing information systems industry. Industry data is culled from secondary sources readily available to decision makers in the real world. The profiles are used, principally, as background information for several Strategy Sessions, but they also serve as examples of the industry overviews that students should build for assigned cases. A template for students to use in gathering information on an industry, as a precursor for other kinds of in-depth analysis, is also included in this part.

Part V consists of two optional semester-long projects, along with a framework (the MICA method) for in-class discussion of strategic management cases—a format that facilitates full-class participation. The projects require field research and decision making by students in teams. The MICA method is an alternative to the standard Socratic approach to case discussion and is designed to generate maximum participation by students in class using a structured format. It is also incorporates a technique for clarifying grading criteria.

Acknowledgements

Credit for making this book really goes first to John Szilagyi, Executive Editor at South-Western. His vision and commitment to a strategic management series provided us with the opportunity to develop this experiential text. Our thanks also go to the other fine professionals at South-Western, namely Judy O'Neill, our developmental editor, and editorial assistant Jennifer Baker, for important contributions relating to the text's content. We would also like to thank James Reidel of LogaTorial Co. for his thoughtful attention in editing and producing this book.

We also wish to acknowledge our reviewers, who read drafts of our work and provided valuable insights and suggestions for its improvement. We are grateful to

Melissa S. Baucus
Utah State University

Phyllis Campbell
Bethel College

Victor Forlani
University of Dayton

Vipin Gupta
University of Pennsylvania

William Guth
New York University

Randall S. Hanson
Stetson University

John Mezias
University of Miami

Jerry Moorman
Mesa State College

David A. O'Dell
McPherson College

John K. Ross III
Southwest Texas State University

Srivatsa Seshadri
University of Nebraska at Kearney

Hebert Sherman
Long Island University

Anne Walsh
La Salle University

Floyd G. Willoughby
Oakland University

Finally, the exercises and projects described herein have benefited from feedback we have received over several semesters from students who have worked with them. We are grateful for their guidance in helping us strike the right chords. However, there is always room for further improvement and we welcome your comments, as they will most definitely help us make *Strategize!* even better for you in the future. Please email us about your experiences or register your comments on the Talk to the Author page at **http://siciliano.swcollege.com**.

Julie I. Siciliano
Western New England College
jsicilia@wnec.edu

C. Gopinath
Suffolk University
cgopinat@acad.suffolk.edu

Strategy Session Matrix for Strategic Mangement Textbooks

The Strategy Sessions are experiential activities designed to give students practice in applying models and concepts from the strategic management course. These exercises can be included when theories are being discussed in class or at other times during the semester to reinforce previously reviewed material. The matrix in Figure I.2 on the facing page shows how the Sessions complement chapter discussions in several traditional strategic management texts.

Figure I.2 Strategy Session Matrix for Selected Strategic Management Texts

Strategy Session	David 7th ed. 1999	Hill & Jones 5th ed. 2001	Hitt & Ireland 4th ed. 2001	Wheelen & Hunger 7th ed. 2000	Harrison & St. John 1998 (Foundations)	Pitts & Lei 2nd ed. 2000	Thompson & Strickland 12th ed. 2001	Grant 3rd ed. 1998	Bourgeois, Duhaime & Stimpert 2nd ed. 1999
1 Decision Making at the Strategic and Operational Level	Ch. 1, 8	Ch. 1, 5	Ch. 5	Ch. 1, 7	Ch. 1, 3, 6	Ch. 1	Ch. 2	Ch. 1	Ch. 1, 2
2 Understanding the Concept of Strategy	Ch. 6	Ch. 1		Ch. 1	Ch. 1		Ch. 1, 2	Ch. 1	Ch. 2
3 Communicating Purpose Through Mission Statements	Ch. 3	Ch. 2	Ch. 1	Ch. 5	Ch. 3	Ch. 1	Ch. 2	Ch. 2	Ch. 6
4 The Board's Role in Corporate Governance	Ch. 6	Ch. 2	Ch. 10	Ch. 2	Ch. 3		Ch. 1	Ch. 6	Ch. 11
5 Viewing Strategy from the Stakeholder Perspective	Ch. 1	Ch. 2	Ch. 1	Ch. 2	Ch. 1	Ch. 1	Ch. 2	Ch. 2	
6 Forces Affecting Competitive Strategy	Ch. 4	Ch. 3	Ch. 4	Ch. 3	Ch. 2	Ch. 2	Ch. 3	Ch. 3	Ch. 4
7 Generating a plan of action—SWOT Analysis	Ch. 6	Ch. 1	Ch. 2, 3	Ch. 3, 4, 5	Ch. 1	Ch. 1, 2, 3	Ch. 4	Ch. 1	Ch. 4
8 Developing Generic Strategy	Ch. 2	Ch. 6	Ch. 4	Ch. 5	Ch. 4	Ch. 4	Ch. 5	Ch. 8, 9	Ch. 7
9 Viewing Corporate Strategy from the Core Competencies Perspective	Ch. 5, 6	Ch. 4, 10	Ch. 3, 6	Ch. 6, 7	Ch. 1, 5	Ch. 6	Ch. 4, 11	Ch. 5, 15, 16	Ch. 3, 9
10 Global Strategic Alliances	Ch. 10	Ch. 9	Ch. 9, 13	Ch. 5, 13	Ch. 4, 5	Ch. 8	Ch. 5, 9	Ch. 11, 14	
11 Identifying Transnational Strategies	Ch. 10	Ch. 8	Ch. 8	Ch. 13	Ch. 8	Ch. 7	Ch. 6	Ch. 14	
12 Understanding Turnaround Management	Ch. 2	Ch. 10	Ch. 7	Ch. 6, 10	Ch. 7	Ch. 5, 6	Ch. 8, 9	Ch. 12	Ch. 9, 12
13 Succeeding in Strategy Formulation and Implementation	Ch. 6, 9	Ch. 6, 9, 11	Ch. 12	Ch. 10	Ch. 4, 5, 7	Ch. 12	Ch. 11	Ch. 1, 12	Ch. 3
14 Structuring to Support Strategy	Ch. 7	Ch. 11	Ch. 11	Ch. 7	Ch. 6	Ch. 9	Ch. 11	Ch. 6	Ch. 10
15 Strategy Implementation Using the 7-S Model	Ch. 7, 8, 9	Ch. 11, 12, 13	Ch. 12	Ch. 8, 9, 10	Ch. 7	Ch. 10, 12	Ch. 12	Ch. 12	Ch. 12
16 The Role of Cooperation in Strategic Management	Ch. 4	Ch. 9	Ch. 9	Ch. 5		Ch. 6, 11	Ch. 5	Ch. 3	
17 Social Responsibility of Corporations	Ch. 1	Ch. 2	Ch. 12	Ch. 2	Ch. 1	Ch. 1	Ch. 2, 13		

Contents

PART IV   INDUSTRY ANALYIS

PART V   SEMESTER PROJECTS

Part I

Understanding Strategic Management

Strategy Session 1

Decision Making at the Strategic and Operational Level

OBJECTIVE

In this session, the concept of strategy is explored by distinguishing it from operational issues. After finishing this reading and performing the accompanying exercise, you will be able to identify strategic and operational-level decisions.

Decisions are constantly made in organizations, and they can broadly be considered to fall in one of two categories. One set of decisions involves the development of strategies for the total organization. These strategic-level decisions include defining the mission and overall corporate goals, determining what businesses to be in and how to compete in those businesses. The second set of decisions helps to make strategic-level decisions work. They keep the business running efficiently by translating strategies into action in the areas of human resources, finance and accounting, marketing, research and development, and manufacturing. When managers of these business functions choose courses of action, they take their cues from the strategies developed for the total organization. Thus, it is important to have a clear understanding of the distinction between strategic and operational decision making, but it is a distinction that is not always easy to make.

At the start of this strategic management course, the typical way that many view the issues will be from an operational perspective. This is a familiar perspective for business majors with courses of study specializing in one function of the business (e.g., marketing, accounting, computer information systems, etc.). Moreover, individuals with professional experience often make decisions dealing with their particular area of expertise at the operational level. However, because strategic decisions affect the firm as a whole and involve creating competitive advantage, the distinction between strategic and operational is an important one. This is not surprising, since up to this point in most curricula, courses are designed around the business functions and provide theory and training at the operational level. Moreover, those individuals with professional experience have tended to be members of a single department focused on a business function. Although more and more organizations encourage employees at all levels to view their areas from a broader and strategic perspective, many have not had the opportunity or training to practice strategic thinking. Even when the conceptual distinction between strategic- and operational-level decision making becomes clear, in reality the line separating the two types of decisions is not always obvious. For example, on the face of it buying a small machine should be considered operational, should it not? But if new equipment is purchased in support of a new *strategic* direction for the firm, is the decision to purchase suddenly strategic in scope? What

> Some people accuse us of taking on too much, but the reality is that we say no to many, many more things than we actually approve. A big part of my role as Chief Yahoo is to filter and prioritize so that we keep our focus.
>
> —Jerry Yang, interview in Fortune

about an aggregated series of operational decisions, such as purchasing several machines in the production area? If equipment purchases can in fact give an organization additional competencies and thereby alter the strategy of the firm, then the answer, perhaps, is yes.

To help clarify what should be viewed as strategic decision making, the following points provide a basis for thinking about issues and decisions from a strategic perspective:

1. Does the decision deal with identifying a new business area—or the future direction of the firm?
2. Does the decision affect the firm as a whole?
3. Does it have a significant financial impact on the firm?
4. Would it evoke a significant response in the environment—that is, from competitors or other stakeholders?

The benefit of distinguishing between the two levels of decision making in the strategic management course is that one begins to develop a type of *strategic thought process*. This helps the strategic manager to recommend decisions that affect the firm as a whole and to better understand the importance of competitive advantage. While effectiveness at both the operational and strategic levels is essential to competitiveness, a focus on operational decisions can result in an organization doing things better than its competitors—improvements in operational performance, however, are often easily imitated.

The strategic-level decisions that focus on doing things *differently* are what provide a sustained competitive advantage where an organization preserves meaningful differences with rivals. By the time this strategic management course is completed, how these strategic-level decisions differ from those involving operational-level issues will not only be understood, it will be appreciated, too, in a completely new way.

 Strategy_Online

Jerry Yang of Yahoo believes that the matrix of decisions is bigger than it used to be, "but we still face the same sorts of issues. Do we invest in branding? Do we invest in people? Do we go to China, or do we go to Brazil?" For more of his views on strategic management and other issues, check out Context Magazine's *archived interview with Jerry Yang:*

http://www.contextmag.com/archives/200004/feature0thenextbigthing.asp

Exercise: Innkeepers of America

INSTRUCTIONS

After reading the case below, read the statements that follow it and put an S next to the decisions that are strategic and an O next to the ones that are operational.

Innkeepers of America, a medium sized national hotel chain, has operated successfully for many years in the economy segment of the lodging industry. Its chain of hotels provides rooms that are comfortable and roomy. To keep costs low, the company locates its properties near a major restaurant instead of providing that service itself. The rooms and lobby areas are comfortable with normal accommodations, but extra frills are avoided. Although the company has its own staff of security guards, cleaning and landscaping services are contracted out to local companies.

During the past three years, several new competitors have entered the economy segment of the industry using aggressive pricing strategies. To meet the new competitive threat, management developed a series of steps that they have followed over the past two years. They lowered the price of the hotel rooms by 10% last year and again this year with the goal of matching competitor prices. They also created a new advertising campaign that targeted budget-conscious customers by giving them discount coupons for weekend stays. This promotion increased occupancy on the weekends, and plans are to continue it this year. Three new positions were created and filled in the customer service department. Employees were given shares of the company stock as part of a bonus plan. A continental breakfast menu was created. Guests could get rolls and breakfast drinks in the lobby or they could get them delivered to their room for an extra fee. Over 50% of the guests used this service. The reservation system was fully computerized, and front-desk employees received four half-day training sessions on the new system. However, despite these changes, the company's overall market share did not increase, and in the last quarter it dropped slightly. The company's net profit margin also declined from the previous year.

Management was concerned, and a meeting was held to recommend and review courses of action. The head of marketing proposed a new company Web site where customers could book reservations online. The operations vice president noted that with the additional customer service staff and features, such as the continental breakfast, the company's image was beginning to change. She recommended that all of the new hotels planned for construction next year be designed with more features to appeal to an upscale market segment. The marketing vice president agreed and noted that an upscale property would allow management to charge higher prices for the rooms to cover the higher costs associated with the upcoming campaigns. The president shared a letter with the group where a major competitor, Economy Lodge, Inc., wanted to merge with Innkeepers of America. According to the president, "This merger would increase our market share by a sizable amount, and we would be able to compete more strongly in the economy segment of this industry. However, before we decide on this and other actions you've recommended, we should rewrite our mission statement so that we have a sense of our core purpose and which decisions we should make to achieve that purpose."

_____1.   Innkeepers of America's position in the economy segment of the lodging industry.

_____2.   Locating properties next to a restaurant rather than have food and beverage in-house.

_____3.   Price of rooms lowered further to meet competition.

_____4.   New advertising campaign with discount coupons for weekend stays.

_____5.   Three new customer service positions.

_____6.   Shares of company stock issued for employee bonuses.

_____7.   Providing continental breakfast in the lobby.

_____8.   Room service (for continental breakfast only).

_____9.   Computerized reservation system.

_____10.   Training program for front-desk employees.

_____11.   Web site where reservations can be booked on line.

_____12.   New hotel properties built with additional features to appeal to an upscale market.

_____13.   Merger with Economy Lodge, Inc.

_____14.   Rewrite mission statement.

_____15.   Contracting cleaning and landscaping services.

Strategy Session 2

Understanding the Concept of Strategy

OBJECTIVE

This session's reading and exercise provide the opportunity to explore strategy from several points of view. Knowing multiple definitions helps in understanding the different facets of the concept.

Strategy is a term used in many ways. The exercise in Strategy Session 1 revealed that strategy can be large decisions that managers make. But even smaller, tactical moves can prove to be strategic in certain cases. Early definitions of strategy were the plans that "matched" the organization to its environment, whereas today the formal definitions describe it as a set of decisions and actions that managers take to achieve organizational goals related to achieving strategic competitiveness and earning above-average returns. In addition, the word *strategic* modifies many other words and actions to give them a sense of importance. For example, we read about a "strategic move" or a major "strategic undertaking." Quite often, the debate on what to do and how it is done occurs because of the different meanings attributed to *strategy*. Henry Mintzberg provides five definitions:

> The field of strategic management cannot afford to rely on a single definition of strategy, indeed the word has long been used implicitly in different ways even if has traditionally been defined formally in only one.
>
> —Henry Mintzberg

Strategy as a plan According to Mintzberg, this is a consciously intended course of action. It could take the form of a set of guidelines or a written report that managers use to guide their decisions. Many years ago, it was common for most large organizations to go through a formal planning process and arrive at a document of what was to be done in the future.

Strategy as a ploy This is a short-term tactic or a maneuver that is intended to outwit a competitor. When software developers announce a new product well before it is ready, they are preempting competition through a ploy.

Strategy as a pattern This is an after-the-fact view of strategy. When we look at organizations over time, as journalists in the business press do, we find that their management's decisions fall into a pattern that suggests a direction. When that direction is not what was originally intended, it is called "emergent."

Strategy as a position Managers see their firm as occupying a space within an environment. This could be defined as market share, or leadership as in General Electric's desire to be in those businesses where the company holds a number one or two position.

Strategy as a perspective This is a way of perceiving the world, and individuals in an organization are united by common thinking and behavior. Hewlett-Packard Company developed the HP way based on its engineering culture. Lucent Technologies claims it makes the things that make communications work.

The different definitions enrich our understanding of how strategies are formed and how the process can be managed. As a plan, strategy provides information about what was intended. As a ploy, the focus is on direct competition and how maneuvers can gain advantage for a firm. As a pattern, strategy looks at actions and behaviors, revealing the unintended or emergent strategies that often occur. As a position, the focus is on the competitive environment and how organizations struggle for survival. As a perspective, strategy looks at how a collective group of individuals share values and behave in such a way that they cooperate in the production of specific goods and services.

These definitions enable us to view strategy not only from the important competitive perspective but also to better understand how organizational members help to shape the process.

 Strategy_Online

Explore the different meanings of strategy in the articles and news links available at The Business Strategy Search Specialist Web site:

http://www.sookoo.com

Exercise: How Do You Define Strategy?

INSTRUCTIONS

Reconsider the Innkeepers of America case on page 5. Read it again if necessary. How do you define strategy in that reading? Do you find evidence of the different forms of strategy in the case? Record the evidence according to the form of strategy in the tables below.

Form of Strategy	Evidence/Actions
Plan	
Ploy	

(Continued on next page)

Form of Strategy	Evidence/Actions
Pattern	
Position	
Perspective	

Strategy Session 3

Communicating Purpose Through Mission Statements

OBJECTIVE

This session shows whether organizations defines their core purpose by simply describing current product lines and the service they provide—or whether they define their core purpose in terms of the customer needs being satisfied. After finishing this reading, perform the exercise and team activity that follows.

The first responsibility of management is to provide a clear sense of direction for decision making and to guide strategy development. In strategic management, an organization's general and enduring sense of direction is defined as its *mission*. The most common way that organizations attempt to communicate their sense of purpose or direction is through a mission statement.

OVERVIEW OF MISSION STATEMENT CRITERIA

Mission statements vary considerably in their design. Two basic criteria, however, define for employees, customers, and all stakeholders the organization's highest and most enduring goals:

1. A statement that defines the organization's core purpose in terms of customer needs.
2. A statement that indicates the key beliefs, values, and priorities that managers are committed to and that influence the decisions they make.

DEFINITION OF THE ORGANIZATION'S CORE PURPOSE

When an organization defines its core purpose, it should make clear the importance people attach to the organization's work. In other words, the organization must define its reason for being.

The mission statement should clearly answer the questions: "What business are we in?" and "What business should we be in?" It is important that these questions be answered in terms of customer needs and not based on the products or services the company currently offers. Some companies make the mistake of simply describing

> Only a clear definition of the mission and purpose of the business makes possible clear and realistic business objectives. It is the foundation for priorities, strategies, plans, and work assignments.
>
> —Peter F. Drucker

their current product lines or customer segments as their core purpose, when instead they should focus on the customer needs that the business seeks to satisfy. To get at a customer-oriented definition, one method is to answer the question *Why?* several times.

A technique for moving from a product or service orientation to a customer-needs definition of an organization's purpose is shown in Table 1.1, with examples using a company that manufacturers cosmetics and a company that provides market research data respectively.

Table 1.1   Mission Statements: Moving from a Product/Service Orientation to a Customer-Needs Orientation

Product/Service Definition	Examples
Instruction: Start with a descriptive statement: "We make x products or we provide x services."	Company that manufactures and markets face makeup: We *make quality cosmetics.* Company that provides market research to other organizations: We *do research about market characteristics and market demand for companies in a variety of industries.*

Customer-Needs Definition	Examples
Instruction: Answer the question *why* as many times as it takes to get to the fundamental purpose of the organization—or the customer-needs definition. That is, why do we make these products or deliver these services? What needs do the products/services satisfy?	**Face Makeup Company** ("We make quality cosmetics.") Why? We *enhance beauty and enable our customers to maintain a youthful appearance.* **Market Research Organization** ("We do research about market characteristics . . .") Why? *To provide the best data available so that the customers will understand their markets better.* Why? *To contribute to our customers' success by helping them understand their markets.*

For many people in a company, it is difficult to think about the organization's purpose in any way other than the product manufactured or the service provided. After all, it is "what we do." Because it is so obvious, it is easier to identify and buy into as the mission. However, this paradigm can be a trap that potentially may keep management focused on outdated products.

CHARTING A STRATEGIC COURSE

Today, many products and services race through the business cycle and are obsolete or outmoded faster than products and services were in the past. For example, once there was only one long-distance telephone service. Now there are long distance "packages" for a range of customer types that, in turn, change their pricing, features, and names from month to month. By being very clear about what the organization stands for and why it exists, decision makers enhance their ability to think strategically about what the organization could do, as well as what it should not do.

Compare the stories of Zenith and Motorola. For many years, both companies were known for manufacturing televisions. While Zenith retained its focus on television manufacturing, Motorola changed from televisions to microprocessors—and then on to aggressively pursuing strategies to achieve its core purpose of providing integrated communication solutions and embedded electronic solutions. Its openness to new technologies to achieve its core purpose vaulted it to one of the best companies in business today. Motorola could give up what it made years ago when it did not fit the core purpose. Zenith could not.

MAKING OPERATIONAL-LEVEL DECISIONS

Mission statements, when they are written in terms of customer needs, also serve as a decision making and leadership tool for operational-level decisions. An example from the government sector illustrates this process. At first glance, a city fire department might define its mission based on what it does: put out fires. But a fire department's purpose goes beyond this definition. If a car is leaking gasoline, or if a parent calls to say his or her child stopped breathing, the fire department will respond and provide life-saving measures and emergency transportation to a hospital. Thus, a more realistic statement based on why the fire department exists would be to ensure the preparation of officers, men, women, and equipment "so that together we are prepared to provide cost effective resolution to emergencies that threaten or will threaten life and property in our community."

Given this new definition—or mission statement—of the city's fire department, suppose the department has limited funds and must choose between purchasing a ladder truck to increase the capabilities of the department and an equipment truck to carry new rescue tools. As part of the decision-making process, the team of firefighters reviews these two options against the statement.

First, the ladder truck: Does it improve the preparedness of the equipment? Yes.

Is it cost effective? Yes, as evident by a review of the financial data.

Will it help to reduce the threat to lives and property? Yes. It will provide access to those who need rescue from upper floors.

The review continues. Then the equipment truck is compared in terms of its value in supporting the department's purpose. The advantage of this process is that the operational-level decision is based on clear facts and is linked to the organization's mission.

Similarly, at AT&T the decision to add new products and services is based largely on the company's customer-oriented mission to bring people together and give them easy access to each other. How closely the proposed product or service achieves this mission determines whether it will be introduced or not.

Thus, in for-profit, nonprofit, and government organizations, a clearly defined purpose written from a customer-oriented perspective has two advantages. It provides a framework for charting an organization's strategic course, and it is a guide for operational-level decision making.

PHILOSOPHY AND VALUES

The second key component of the mission statement defines the organization's philosophy—its basic beliefs, values, and priorities. These statements also provide guidelines for those within the company, particularly in terms of behaviors, their conduct, how they intend to do business, and what kind of organization they want to build. An understanding of the organization's social responsibility is also spelled out.

A company whose values are legendary is Johnson & Johnson. This organization publishes a value statement—a *credo*—that expresses its belief that the company's first responsibility is to the doctors, nurses, and patients who use Johnson & Johnson products. Next, come its employees, the communities in which the employees live and work, and finally the stockholders. The credo is displayed in every manager's office, and it guides making every important decision.

 Strategy_Online

For a copy of the credo, view the Johnson & Johnson Web site at:

http://www.johnsonandjohnson.com

Exercise: How Well Do These Organizations Communicate Their Purpose?

INSTRUCTIONS

Review the mission statements of Harley-Davidson, American United Life Insurance Company, and Continental Airlines in Table 1.2. Each provides a definition of the company's purpose. Circle the number rating in questions 1–6 that most closely matches how you think the statements satisfy the criteria for defining the core purpose in terms of customer needs and how the statements express the organization's philosophy and values. Then, as a team, perform activities 7–11.

Table 1.2   Sample Mission Statements

Harley-Davidson		Continental Airlines	
Mission		**Corporate Vision**	
We fulfill dreams through the experience of motorcycling, by providing to motorcyclists and to the general public an expanding line of motorcycles and branded products and services in selected market segments.		To Be Recognized as the Best Airline in the industry by our Customers, Employees and Shareholders.	
American United Life Insurance Company			
Mission	**Values**	**Objectives**	
The mission of AUL is to provide security and peace of mind to our customers by offering insurance and other financial products and services. We will be the company of choice by providing value and building the highest level of trust with our customers.	*Achievement* We will be one of the top companies in the financial services industry. *Stewardship* We will always be strong in order to keep our long-term promise to pay. *Partnership* We will work together as a team with our producers to serve our customers. *Integrity* We will act with the highest ethical standards. *Responsiveness* We will listen to our customers and respond to their needs. *Excellence* We will be distinguished as a quality company and good corporate citizen.	*Customer* Maximize the value to our customers by providing superior quality in products and services. *Growth* Grow revenue and assets on a profitable basis. Increase our number of customers. *Partners* Grow and strengthen our partnerships. *People* Cultivate an environment that values, develops and retains high-quality people.	

HARLEY-DAVIDSON

1. How closely does the mission statement define Harley-Davidson's core purpose in terms of customer needs?

1	2	3
No core purpose discussed	Defines core purpose in terms of product/service provided	Defines core purpose very well in terms of customer needs

2. Are statements of the organization's philosophy and values included?

1	2	3
No statements of philosophy/values		Clearly expresses corporate philosophy/values

CONTINENTAL AIRLINES

3. How closely does the mission statement define Continental Airline's core purpose in terms of customer needs?

1	2	3
No core purpose discussed	Defines core purpose in terms of product/services provided	Defines core purpose very well in terms of customer needs

4. Are statements of the organization's philosophy and values included?

1	2	3
No statements of philosophy/values	Statements are vague	Clearly expresses corporate philosophy/values

AMERICAN UNITED LIFE INSURANCE COMPANY

5. How closely does the mission statement define American United Life Insurance Company's core purpose in terms of customer needs?

1	2	3
No core purpose discussed	Defines core purpose in terms of product/service provided	Defines core purpose very well in terms of customer needs

6. Are statements of the organization's philosophy and values included?

1	2	3
No statements of philosophy/values	Statements are vague	Clearly expresses corporate philosophy/values

TEAM ACTIVITY: MISSION STATEMENT REVISION

Names: _____

_____

7. Transfer each team member's ratings onto the charts below:

Team Member	Core Purpose			Philosophy and Values		
	Harley-Davidson	Continental Airlines	American United Life	Harley-Davidson	Continental Airlines	American United Life

8. Discuss the above individual ratings. Through consensus, develop a new team rating of a 1, 2, or 3 for each of the mission statements.

Core Purpose			Philosophy and Values		
Harley-Davidson	Continental Airlines	American United Life	Harley-Davidson	Continental Airlines	American United Life

9. Rewrite one of the company statements to incorporate an improved definition of the core purpose according to the customer needs criteria.

_____

_____

_____

_____

_____

_____

_____

_____

_____

10. Pick one of the company statements that could include more information regarding philosophy and values. Give examples of what might be included.

_____

_____

_____

_____

_____

_____

_____

_____

_____

_____

_____

_____

11. What other characteristics of the statements did your team notice/discuss?

_____

_____

_____

_____

_____

_____

_____

_____

_____

_____

Strategy Session 4

The Board's Role in Corporate Governance

OBJECTIVE

This session develops an understanding of the key issues involved in the governance of a corporation. Typically, in the study of strategic management, the focus is on the role of the CEO. The Board of Directors has important roles to play as well, and an understanding of these roles provides a necessary element in understanding the corporation as a whole.

The focus in strategic management is always on the CEO. This individual is taken to represent the top management of the enterprise, charged with the formulation and implementation of strategy. However, the CEO is answerable to the owners of the enterprise, namely the shareholders. The Board of Directors, who are elected to oversee the affairs of the corporation, represent the shareholders. Thus, an examination of the role of the Board and the relationship of the CEO to the Board are important for an understanding of the strategic management of the firm.

The governing board of directors must be a board that represents no one except the basic long-term interests of the enterprise.

—Peter F. Drucker

BOARD ROLES

The Board may be said to perform three roles in the governance of the firm:

1. **Control** This role is internally focused and is derived from its position as representatives of the owners. Agency theory suggests that in a principal-agent relationship, the agent's interests may diverge from that of the principal and needs to be controlled. Thus the board serves as a watchdog over management, a role that includes monitoring managerial competence and overseeing resource allocation.

2. **Service** This role has an external focus and considers the board as *boundary spanners*. That is, they serve to connect the organization to its environment by providing information to management on the one hand, and represent the firm to the community on the other. As suggested by stakeholder theory, the board enhances the firm's legitimacy.

3. **Strategy** This role is more recent in origin. Institutional theory suggests that organizations develop an inner logic of their own and seek a position and purpose different from that of those who control them. For this reason the board needs to think in terms of the long-term strategy of an enterprise, even though it may not always serve the purpose of the diverse group of owners who may seek short-term rewards.

In seeking to perform these three roles, different boards have taken to different paths. Some boards are activists and others are more passive. During the late 1980s and early 1990s, several large corporations went through a difficult period of governance leading to disagreements between the board and the CEO. The CEOs of General Motors, IBM, Kmart, Goodyear Tire & Rubber Co., Abbott Laboratories, and Greyhound Lines, among others, had to quit over their differences with the Board on how the company was run. The debate over corporate governance issues resulted in the National Association of Corporate Directors announcing guidelines in November 1996 in order to enhance the professionalism of board members. These include becoming active participants and decision makers in the boardroom and not merely passive advisers, limiting the number of board memberships, and immersing themselves in the company's business and industry.

 Strategy_Online

For more information on corporate governance issues, navigate your Web browser to the Web site of the Institute of Chartered Accountants in England and Wales, whose Corporate Governance Committee develops the Institute's views and policies on this issue:

http://www.icaew.co.uk/depts/td/tdcgg/cgg001.htm

LENS, Inc. provides several corporate governance links at their Web site, which also provide excellent supplementary readings:

http://www.lens-inc.com/links.html

Exercise: Translating the Board's Role into Guidelines for Practice

INSTRUCTIONS

There are two parts to this exercise. Part I involves reviewing a listing of Board of Director guidelines and asks you to identify the Board's role or roles associated with each guideline.

In Part II, review the Disney Corporation Board's composition and how it relates to the guidelines.

PART I: BOARD GUIDELINES

Read the following guidelines adopted by the Board of Directors of General Motors:

- Assign, for each item below, one or more of the three roles (Control, Service and Strategy) identified for the board in the accompanying reading. Circle the appropriate role(s).

- Do any of the items infringe on what you would consider top management's prerogative in running the company? Make notes.

- Are there any areas of governance of a corporation not considered that you would wish to include? Write a brief statement to be added to the guidelines in the space provided at the end of the exercise.

GM BOARD GUIDELINES

Selection and Composition of the Board

1. *Board Membership Criteria*

The Committee on Director Affairs is responsible for reviewing with the Board on an annual basis the appropriate skills and characteristics required of Board members in the context of the current makeup of the Board. This assessment should include issues of diversity, age, skills such as understanding of manufacturing technologies, international background, etc.—all in the context of an assessment of the perceived needs of the Board at that point in time.

Control	Service	Strategy

2. *Selection and Orientation of New Directors*

The Board itself should be responsible in fact as well as in procedure for selecting its own members. The Board delegates the screening process involved to the Committee on Director Affairs with the direct input from the Chairman of the Board as well as the Chief Executive Officer.

Control	Service	Strategy

Board Leadership

3. *Selection of Chairman and CEO*

The Board should be free to make this choice any way that seems best for the company at a given point in time. Therefore, the Board does not have a policy one way or the other on whether or not the role of the Chief Executive and Chairman should be separate and, if it is to be separate, whether the Chairman should be selected from the non-employee Directors or be an employee.

Control	Service	Strategy

Board Composition and Performance

4. *Mix of Management and Independent Directors*

The Board believes that there should be a majority of independent Directors on the GM Board. The Board is willing to have members of Management, in addition to the Chief Executive Officer, as Directors. On matters of corporate governance, the Board assumes decisions will be made by the outside directors.

Control	Service	Strategy

5. *Board Definition of What Constitutes Independence for Directors*

The Board believes there is no current relationship between any outside director and GM that would be construed in any way to compromise any Board member being designated independent.

Control	Service	Strategy

6. *Former Chief Executive Officer's Board Membership*

The Board believes this is a matter to be decided in each individual instance. It is assumed that when the Chief Executive Officer resigns from that position, he/she should offer his/her resignation from the Board at the same time. Whether the individual continues to serve on the Board is a matter for discussion at that time with the new Chief Executive Officer and the Board.

Control	Service	Strategy

7. Directors Who Change Their Present Job Responsibility

Individual directors who change the responsibility they held when they were elected to the Board should submit a letter of resignation to the Board. There should be an opportunity for the Board via the Committee on Director Affairs to review the continued appropriateness of Board membership under these circumstances.

Control	Service	Strategy

8. Term Limits

The Board does not believe it should establish term limits. As an alternative to term limits, the Committee on Director Affairs, in conjunction with the Chief Executive Officer will formally review each Director's continuation on the Board every five years. This will also allow each Director the opportunity to conveniently confirm his/her desire to continue as a member of the Board.

Control	Service	Strategy

9. Assessing the Board's Performance

The Committee on Director Affairs is responsible to report annually to the Board an assessment of the Board's performance. This assessment should be of the Board's contribution as a whole and specifically review areas in which the Board and/or the Management believe a better contribution could be made.

Control	Service	Strategy

10. Interaction with Institutional Investors, Press, Customers, etc.

The Board believes that the Management speaks for General Motors. Individual Board members may, from time to time, at the request of management meet or otherwise communicate with various constituencies that are involved with General Motors.

Control	Service	Strategy

Board Relationship to Senior Management

11. *Board Access to Senior Management*

Board members have complete access to GM's Management. It is assumed that Board members will use judgment to be sure that this contact is not distracting to the business operation of the Company and that such contact, if in writing, be copied to the Chief Executive and the Chairman of the Executive Committee.

Control	Service	Strategy

Meeting Procedures

12. *Selection of Agenda Items for Board Meetings*

The Chairman of the Board/ Chief Executive Officer will establish the agenda for each Board meeting. Each Board member is free to suggest the inclusion of item(s) on the agenda.

Control	Service	Strategy

13. *Board Materials Distributed in Advance*

Information and data that are important to the Board's understanding of the business must be distributed in writing to the Board before the Board meets. The Management will make every attempt to see that this material is as brief as possible while still providing the desired information.

Control	Service	Strategy

Committee Matters

14. *Number, Structure, and Independence of Committees*

The current committee structure of the Company seems appropriate. The current six Committees are Audit, Capital Stock, Director Affairs, Executive, Executive Compensation, Investment Funds, and Public Policy. Except for the Investment Funds Committee, committee membership will consist only of independent directors.

Control	Service	Strategy

Leadership Development

15. *Formal Evaluation of the Chief Executive Officer*

The full Board (independent directors) should make this evaluation annually, and it should be communicated to the Chief Executive Officer by the Chairman of the Executive Committee.

The evaluation should be based on objective criteria including performance of the business, accomplishment of long-term strategic objectives, development of Management, etc.

Control	Service	Strategy

- **Are all aspects of the Board's role clearly spelled out in the guidelines shown in this exercise?**
- **Are there any areas of governance of a corporation not considered in these guidelines? Note your observations here.**

_____

_____

_____

_____

_____

_____

_____

_____

_____

PART II: DISNEY BOARD

Table 4.1 lists the names of the Directors of the Disney Corporation Board as of 1998 and gives a brief background information for each. Review the list and respond to the questions that follow.

1. Identify the possible contribution to the three roles of the board that these Directors might make.

Table 4.1   Board members of the Disney Corporation, 1998

Alphabetical Listing of Board Members	Role Control/Service/Strategy
Reveta F. Bowers, 48: Head of school for the Center for Early Education, where Mr. Eisner's children attended classes. (1993)	
Roy E. Disney, 56. Vice Chairman, head of animation department. (1967)	
Michael D. Eisner, 54: Chairman and Chief Executive. (1984)	
Stanley P. Gold, 54: President and Chief Executive of Shamrock Holdings, Inc., which manages about $1 billion in investments for the Disney family. (1984)	
Sanford M. Litvack, 60: Senior executive vice president.	
Ignacio E. Loranzo Jr., 69: Chairman of Loranzo Enterprises, publisher of La Opinion newspaper in Los Angeles. (1981)	
George J. Mitchell, 63: Washington D.C. attorney, former United States Senator. Disney paid Mr. Mitchell $50,000 for his consulting on international business matters in fiscal 1996. His Washington law firm was paid an additional $122,764. (1995)	
Thomas S. Murphy, 71: Former chairman and chief executive of Capital Cities/ABC Inc. (1996)	
Richard A. Nunis, 64: Chairman of Walt Disney attractions. (1981)	

Table 4.1   Board members of the Disney Corporation, 1998 (cont.)

Alphabetical Listing of Board Members	Role Control/Service/Strategy
The Rev. Leo J. O'Donovan, 62: President of Georgetown University, where one of Mr. Eisner's children attended college. Mr. Eisner sat on the Georgetown board and has contributed more than $1 million to the school. (1996)	
Sidney Poitier, 69: The celebrated actor, who has starred in numerous films. He won an Academy Award in 1963. (1994)	
Irwin E. Russell, 70: Beverly Hills, Calif. Attorney whose clients include Mr. Eisner. (1987)	
Robert A. M. Stern, 57: New York Architect who designed numerous Disney projects. Mr. Stern received $168,278 for those services in fiscal 1996. (1992)	
E. Cardon Walker, 80: Disney chairman and chief executive, 1980–1983. Received payments totaling $609,826 in fiscal 1996 with respect to films he invested in between 1963 and 1969 under a company incentive plan. (1960)	
Raymond L. Watson, 70: Disney chairman in 1983 and 1984. (1974)	
Gary L. Wilson, 56: Disney Chief Financial Officer, 1985–1989; now cochairman of Northwest Airlines. (1985)	

2. Evaluate the board using the GM guidelines. Do you see this board as satisfying or not satisfying any of them? (Note: The date within the parenthesis indicates the year the member joined the Board.)

_____

_____

_____

Strategy Session 5

Viewing Strategy from the Stakeholder Perspective

OBJECTIVE

This session illustrates the claims of various stakeholder groups. In the exercise that follows the introductory reading, identify Microsoft's stakeholders—and demonstrate how stakeholder interests and power are part of the strategy process.

Stakeholders are the individuals and groups who have the potential to influence the performance of an organization and who are impacted by the firm's strategies. The traditional concept of business gives supreme importance to the role and interests of the investors or *stock*holders. However, the concept of *stake*holders provides a useful alternative formulation for understanding how numerous organizations, groups, and individuals affect and are affected by a company's strategies and its performance. Examples of stakeholders in a

The stakeholder approach is about groups and individuals who can affect the organization, and is about managerial behavior taken in response to those groups and individuals.

—R. E. Freeman

company include customers and, of course, stockholders. However, employees, creditors, suppliers, governments—and the local community are stakeholders in the company as well. Starbucks, the coffee store chain based in Seattle, is a good example of a company that identifies stakeholders beyond the organization. Its "Starbucks Gives Back" policy states that people

. . . at all levels of the company support Starbucks guiding principle to contribute positively to our communities and our environment.

The relationship of an organization with its stakeholders can be viewed as one of mutual interdependence. Customers provide the organizations with revenue in exchange for products and services. Stockholders buy shares and thus provide capital in exchange for a return on their investment. Employees provide the skills and labor and get income, good working conditions, and job satisfaction. Creditors provide loans and in exchange receive interest payments. Suppliers provide the inputs and receive payment for the inputs. Governments set rules and regulations that maintain fair competition and in exchange expect companies to adhere to the rules. The local community provides an infrastructure and expects the organization to be a socially responsible citizen.

Although managers must view the impact of these relationships when developing strategy, an organization cannot always satisfy the claims of all of its stakeholders. This is particularly the case when the goals of different groups conflict. For example, the local community may ask for a percentage of profits to be donated to local causes. However, stockholders might expect dividends to be paid from extra profits. Alternatively, employees may demand higher wages, while customers look for lower prices.

Because of these potential conflicts, managers are compelled to identify and prioritize stakeholders. The ultimate goal is to develop strategies that assure the achievement of organizational goals while maintaining positive stakeholder relations.

 Strategy_Online

Starbucks Corporation views its stakeholders as partners. For a look at its various community programs and environmental activities, go to the Starbucks.com Web site and check out the links under the "Company" heading.

www.starbucks.com

Exercise: Role Playing Microsoft Corporation Stakeholder Interests and Power

INSTRUCTIONS

Read this case about the U.S. versus Microsoft Corporation and then complete the following form to develop a preassessment of the Microsoft case. Then perform the team exercise that follows.

U.S. VERSUS MICROSOFT CORPORATION

On October 19, 1998, the U.S. Justice Department and 19 states brought suit against Microsoft Corporation for violating federal antitrust laws and abusing its monopoly power by illegally tying sales of its Internet Explorer browser to its Windows operating system. The Justice Department maintained it used its monopoly power and muscle to crush its competition and in doing so caused harm to consumers.

During the next year, a courtroom battle took place in which 26 witnesses provided viewpoints from both sides. Documentation included two million pages. Thousands of Microsoft email messages were reprinted that, at times, made company employees look greedy, ruthless, and dishonest. Microsoft's position was that the company was a tough but legal competitor and that its innovations had fueled the nation's technology boom. This boom benefited not only the economy but consumers as well. What the government witnesses described as illegal coercion, Microsoft saw as hard bargaining and commonplace business deals.

The central issue for Judge Thomas Penfield Jackson was whether Microsoft limited alternative choices of personal computers (PCs) to consumers by illegally bullying or crushing rivals or whether the company demonstrated aggressive and efficient competition in the dynamic and changing high-tech industry.

In a step that is unusual for antitrust cases, the judge disclosed initial "findings of fact" in a preliminary ruling on November 5, 1999. According to Judge Jackson, Microsoft Corp. had used its monopoly power not only to stifle innovation in the industry but also to harm competition and consumers. Then, on June 7, 2000, the final ruling was issued. Criticizing Microsoft as "untrustworthy," Jackson ordered Microsoft to be split into two companies to lessen the company's monopoly power. Although the judge professed great respect for Microsoft, calling it successful and beneficial to economic enterprise, he noted that the software giant continued to engage in the actions that brought it to trial two years earlier. He cited new email evidence that Microsoft CEO Bill Gates suggested altering some of his dominant software in a way that would damage users of Palm Pilot, a competitive product.

Background and Evidence

In 1994, after Netscape introduced Navigator, its Web browser, it became evident to Microsoft that this new product would be a serious threat to Microsoft. Not only was the product popular, but other companies could bypass Microsoft's operating system and write their software directly for the browser. This was possible through Sun Microsystems Java programming language that was designed to run within a "Java Virtual Machine," and not under an operating system like Windows, Macintosh OS, or Unix. The Java Virtual Machine was a computer program that formed a type of bridge between the Java programming language and the operating system. Once a program was written in the Java language, it could run anywhere. "Write once, run any-where" became the Java motto. Netscape licensed the Java software to include a Java Virtual Machine as part of their web browser. Additionally, Netscape and Sun collaborated on another programming language, called "Javascript," in which people could write small programs to run in the Netscape browser, again regardless of the operating system.

Microsoft reacted in 1995 by proposing a special relationship with Netscape in which Navi-gator would be absorbed into Windows. When Netscape refused the partnership, Microsoft withheld important technical information that delayed Netscape's second browser release and bundled its own browser, Internet Explorer, with Windows. As one Microsoft executive wrote, "Netscape never gets a chance."

According to the government, similar actions were taken against Intel, Apple, and America Online (AOL). Intel was held back. When Intel set its own software standard, Native Signal Processing (NSP), Microsoft's Bill Gates warned Intel CEO Andy Grove that Microsoft would cut support for PCs using Intel's microprocessors. "If Intel is not sticking to its part of the deal," wrote Gates in an e-mail, "let me know." Intel, in due course, stopped work on NSP. Ap-ple was threatened, too. When Apple chose Navigator as its default browser, Gates told then CEO, Gil Amelio, he was going to cancel Microsoft's all-important Mac Office software. Under Steve Jobs, Apple made Explorer its default browser. AOL was closely watched. When AOL agreed to offer Internet Explorer in exchange for a folder on the Windows desktop, Microsoft scrutinized AOL closely to ensure that Netscape was not offered anywhere on its online service.

Other examples were brought before the court. When Compaq signed an agreement to replace a Microsoft Network icon with an AOL icon on the desktops of its PCs, Microsoft threatened to withdraw Compaq's license to install the Windows operating system. Again, another company buckled to this pressure. Compaq restored the MSN icon and then was rewarded with a signifi-cantly lower price for Windows. When Intuit began offering Navigator with its Quicken software, Gates reported in an email, "I told him (the Intuit CEO) frankly that if he had a favor we could do for him that would cost us something like $1 million in return for switching browsers . . . I would be open to doing that." Intuit switched to Internet Explorer a year later. In 1995 Microsoft li-censed Sun's Java technology and produced its own proprietary version of Java that works only on Windows. In 1998, in a separate case, a judge ordered Microsoft to make its code compliant.

The Issues

The judge's findings of fact in the case dealt with four issues: monopoly, attempted collusion, linking products, and exclusionary contracts.

Monopoly   Companies holding more than 70% market share generally are considered to have monopoly power. While the existence of monopoly power by itself does not automatically mean a violation of antitrust laws, misuse of the power is a violation. The government argued that more than 90% of new Intel-based PCs are shipped with a version of Windows pre-installed. Microsoft responded that its dominant position in the market is constantly being threatened by competitors such as the rejuvenated Apple Computer Corp. and new technologies such as Linux and Java. Nonetheless, the court found that "Microsoft enjoys so much power in the market for Intel-compatible PC operating systems that if it wished to exercise this power solely in terms of price, it could charge a price for Windows substantially above that which could be charged in a competitive market."

Attempted Collusion   Providing collusion requires evidence that leaves no doubt as to intent. In a 1984 case involving the airline industry, the government had a tape recording of one executive trying to persuade an executive of another company to set prices. In the Microsoft case, the government argued that at a meeting on June 21, 1995, Microsoft met with Netscape to make an illegal offer to split the market for browser software. Microsoft claimed this was a routine gathering of the software industry, and the company attended mainly to learn the newcomer's business plans and seek areas of cooperation between the two companies. The court noted that although discussions ended before Microsoft was "compelled to demarcate precisely where the boundary between its platform and Netscape's applications would lie, it is unclear whether Netscape's acceptance of Microsoft's proposal would have left the firm with even the ability to survive as an independent business."

Linking products   A federal appeals court ruled in June 1998, as part of a separate earlier case, that Microsoft should be free to bundle its browser with the Windows package as long as it can make a reasonable claim that this action benefits business efficiency or consumers. However, in the current case, the government argued that Microsoft actually harmed consumers by linking its Internet browser (a separate product) to its Windows operating system (the monopoly product) because this stifled competition, and greater competition benefits consumers. Microsoft maintained that the browser was not a separate product but a feature of the operating system. Its business strategy was to continually add new features to the operating system, helping consumers make computers easier to use. The judge believed the government's argument that when the browser was bundled with Windows, the operating system was more likely to crash and was more vulnerable to break-ins by computer hackers. The judge concluded "the preferences of consumers and the responsive behavior of software firms demonstrate that Web browsers and operating systems are separate products."

Exclusionary contracts   Previous court decisions involving other antitrust cases suggest that contracts excluding rivals from 30 or 40 percent of a market are illegal. However, the Supreme Court in 1985 set a strict precedent that if a company has a powerful monopoly position, a contract is illegal if it unnecessarily excludes or handicaps competitors. The government alleged that Microsoft illegally used its power to get Compaq and American Online into agreements that prohibited them from either distributing or promoting Netscape's Navigator. Microsoft maintained that none of its agreements stopped Netscape from distributing its browser, including direct downloading by consumers over the Internet. However, Judge Jackson found that the way Microsoft dealt with Compaq in 1996 and 1997 demonstrated that Microsoft was willing to make special valuable deals when a company agreed to stop distributing or promoting Netscape's Navigator.

The Final Ruling

Judge Jackson's final ruling calls for a breakup of Microsoft into two companies. The Operating System company will get assets and technology to Windows and all future versions, plus a one-time source-code license for Internet Explorer. The Applications company will get Office and everything else, including full Internet Explorer rights, Internet content and Web properties such as MSN, Hotmail, and Expedia. The two companies

a) Cannot enter into any joint venture with one another;

b) Cannot enter into any agreement under which one company develops, sells, licenses or distributes products or services for the other company;

c) Cannot provide technical information or communications interfaces that are not simultaneously made available to other companies; and

d) Cannot license, sell or provide any product or service to one another on terms more favorable than those available to another company. The split into two companies will last 10 years.

The Justice Department announced it would ask the Supreme Court directly to review the order, skipping the usual appeals process. This step is usually reserved for the legal system's most important and urgent cases, and Jackson indicated he would approve the Justice Department's request.

Bill Gates said Microsoft would appeal Jackson's decision immediately and ask a higher court to block all of parts of the ruling while the case is argued. Microsoft also will oppose the Justice Department's request to bypass the federal appeals court in Washington, where Microsoft won a key ruling in 1998.

Microsoft Case: Preassessment

1. After reading the case U.S. versus Microsoft Corporation, what strategy should Microsoft pursue at this time and why?

_____

_____

_____

_____

_____

_____

_____

_____

_____

_____

_____

2. Identify as many stakeholders of Microsoft Corporation as you can. List them according to the level of influence they exert over the company, showing the stakeholder with the highest level first, then the stakeholder with the next highest level of influence, and so on. The last stakeholder on the list should be the one with the lowest level of influence.

_____

_____

_____

_____

_____

_____

_____

_____

_____

_____

_____

_____

TEAM ACTIVITY: STAKEHOLDER GROUP

Names:_____

_____

You will be assigned to a stakeholder group. Each group develops a specific position on what Microsoft Corporation's strategy should be while management formulates its strategic plan.

1. Each stakeholder group should select one person to act as spokesperson while the management team should divide responsibilities among its various members (30 to 40 minutes for steps 1 and 2).

2. The entire class reconvenes with each stakeholder group staying intact. The Microsoft management team presents its plan and answers any questions of clarification. Then the stakeholder groups huddle individually for 5 minutes to review their positions in light of the Microsoft presentation. A spokesperson from each group gives a brief response to the strategic plan. The management in turn is allowed to respond in a very brief manner. The government should have the final say in its role as the group to which management has become primarily accountable. Once all of the stakeholder groups have presented, a question and answer period directed to the management team is in order (40 to 45 minutes).

3. A second brief round of meetings takes place. Microsoft's management team should reassess its strategic plan in light of the critiques by various groups. Each stakeholder group should discuss its position in relationship to the corporation as well as other stakeholder groups (10 minutes).

4. The entire class reconvenes. Microsoft management presents any changes in its strategic plan. Each stakeholder is given an opportunity to make a brief statement. The government should have the final say (10 to 15 minutes).

Part II

Designing Strategy

Strategy Session 6

Forces Affecting Competitive Strategy

OBJECTIVE

This session will help identify the forces of competition and determine what effects these forces have on a competitor's ability to earn high profits. The exercise features a profile of the gaming industry that lets you assess these forces.

An *industry* is defined as the group of competitors that produce similar products or services that satisfy the same basic consumer need. For example, the lodging industry consists of hotels and motels that compete with one another to provide accommodation for travelers away from home. The automobile industry consists of competitors that manufacture and market cars, trucks, and other kinds of vehicles to transport people, property, and services.

Managers must understand the nature of competition within their industry so that they can identify opportunities and threats facing the company. From this analysis, they ultimately determine the best strategy for the firm to pursue to either offset or influence competitive forces. The model for analyzing an industry consists of five forces of competition developed by Michael Porter and a sixth force to incorporate the influence of other stakeholders.

Industry Competition-Rivalry Among Existing Firms   When companies in the same industry compete, they often use tactics such as price competition, new product introduction, and advertising slogans and campaigns. The intensity of the competition depends on factors such as the number of competitors, rate of industry growth, amount of fixed costs, product or service characteristics, exit barriers, capacity levels, and the diversity of rivals.

> *Most of us never recognize opportunity until it goes to work in our competitor's business.*
>
> —P. L. Andarr

Bargaining Power of Suppliers   Suppliers to an industry are those who supply materials and services required by firms in the industry. Suppliers can affect the profitability of an industry if they are able to raise prices or reduce the quality of purchased goods or services. Forces affecting supplier bargaining power include the number of available suppliers, the uniqueness of a supplier's product or service, whether the industry competitor has the potential of integrating backward to produce the supplier's product, the cost to change suppliers, and whether the industry is an important customer of the supplier.

Relative Power of Other Stakeholders   Other stakeholders, such as local communities, creditors, trade associations, governments, special-interest groups, and stockholders can exert powerful influence on the industry and affect the nature of competition.

Threat of New Entrants   New entrants or companies that are not currently part of the competitive group may be looking for an opportunity to enter the industry. How much of a threat they pose depends on the barriers to entry present and the reaction from existing competitors. Barriers to entry include economies of scale, product differentiation, capital requirements, cost disadvantages independent of size, access to distribution channels, and government policy.

Threat of Substitute Products and Services   Substitute products are those provided by competitors in a different industry but come close to satisfying the same consumer need. For example, renting videos is a substitute for going to the movies, wine is a substitute for beer, and so on. The threat of substitutes exists because their existence places a ceiling on prices the industry can charge. When prices get too high, consumers will switch to the substitute, unless the industry upgrades or differentiates its product, thus making the substitute less appealing.

Bargaining Power of Buyers   Buyers are usually consumers of the product or service but buyers can also include wholesalers and retailers who bring the product to the consumer. Buyers affect an industry by being able to force down prices, bargain for more services, or play competitors against each other. Typically, industrial or commercial buyers have bargaining power when they purchase in large volume or when the costs of switching from one industry player to another are low. Consumer buyers tend to be more price sensitive when they purchase undifferentiated products or when the products are expensive relative to their income.

In scanning the industry, management assesses each force as high, medium, or low in terms of its strength. While a high force is a threat because it is likely to reduce profits, a low force is an opportunity because it may allow the company to raise prices and thus earn higher profits.

 Strategy_Online

Graduate and undergraduate business policy and strategic management learners should visit the Strategic Management Club Online (SMCO). This free, user-friendly Web resource provides strategic planning tools, templates, links, and information that help analyze cases and prepare professional-looking reports for class. This web site saves time in performing case research, preparing matrices—and job hunting:

www.strategyclub.com

Exercise: Intensity of Competition in the Gaming Industry

INSTRUCTIONS

Read the description of the gaming industry below. Respond to the questions that follow in order to evaluate the intensity of the forces and their impact on the profitability that can be attained in the industry.

THE GAMING INDUSTRY: TIMES OF EXPANSION AND COMPETITION

The gaming industry includes revenues from wagers at race and dog tracks, lotteries, casinos, legal bookmaking, card rooms and Indian reservations. Over the last 15 years, the U.S. gaming industry has more than tripled in size, due to geographical expansion into new regions during the late 1980s and early 1990s, such as the riverboat casinos of the Midwest and South, and the development of older markets such as Las Vegas and Atlantic City. Casino gambling accounts for more than 75% of all legalized gambling revenues, far ahead of second place Indian reservation gambling at approximately 9%. Despite the past growth in this industry, several challenges now exist for casino companies that are likely to result in lower profits. These include reduced openings of new geographic markets, the major expansion that occurred in Las Vegas in the form of megafacilities, and a new form of competition through Internet gambling sites.

The reduction in geographic expansion has been because fewer states have approved casino type gambling. As of July 1999, the last major new approval of gaming by a state legislature occurred in Indiana in mid-1993. In addition, gaming proposals have been rejected in Florida and Texas. Although statewide approval has not been granted, Michigan voters approved a referendum for the development of up to three casinos in Detroit in November 1996, with the first opened in July 1999.

Because of this slowdown in gaming approvals in new states, growth has occurred in developed locations, with Las Vegas and Atlantic City leading the way. As of mid-1999, there were approximately 235 casinos in Las Vegas in the category of casinos with annual gaming revenue of at least $1 million. Atlantic City is next with 12 high-volume gaming facilities. Six states in the South and Midwest have expanded the number of riverboat casinos, and there are now more than 50 limited-stakes casinos in Colorado and South Dakota. The number of casinos operated on Native American land has increased to 160.

The growth in developed, rather than new, locations has forced operators to find ways to make their facilities unique. Special themes and attractions are ways to differentiate one casino from the next. For example, the Las Vegas Strip has casinos set in ancient Egypt, a pirate ship, and a medieval castle. Some casinos focus on groups of customers by geographic region, such as Boyd Gaming, which targets residents of Hawaii. Other casinos place an emphasis on either high-stakes players or they target low-stakes players, where slot machines are the primary activity.

Through the 1990s, marginal competitors disappeared, and mergers and acquisitions reshaped the industry into five or six dominant players. In 1996, when Hilton began a hostile takeover of ITT Corporation, ITT merged with Starwood Lodging Corporation and Starwood Lodging Trust Corporation. The new firm, Starwood/ITT, became one of the world's largest hotel and gaming corporations. Hilton Hotels remained the next largest competitor with approximately 40% of operating revenues from gaming operations. Harrah's Entertainment, Inc., Mirage Resorts, Circus Circus, Trump Hotel and Casino, Inc., and MGM Grand form the next group of competitors. These are primarily engaged in the gaming industry. In March 2000, MGM Grand announced it would buy Mirage Resorts, Inc., thus continuing the consolidation trend of this industry.

Another characteristic of the gaming industry is the increase in joint ventures, typically between a large gaming company and a group of local partners. Different assets, such as real estate ownership, access to capital, management experience, and political connections are combined in these alliances. The growth of Native American-owned casinos is also creating opportunities for casino companies that cannot own Native American facilities—but do manage them under contract instead.

A new form of competition exists in the gaming industry in the form of Internet betting. Some demand for gambling may be siphoned off by net Internet sites; however, long-term effects of this form of gambling will depend on the likelihood of it being controlled or deterred by regulation. Currently, casino operators must comply with extensive gaming regulations, either at the state or county level. These regulations require extensive reporting. The laws, regulations, and supervisory procedures are concerned with preventing unsuitable persons from having influence or involvement with gaming. Additional regulations cover the maintenance of controls over financial practices of licensees. The decentralized nature of the Internet, however, and its global reach make it difficult for law enforcement officials to have access to records of Internet site usage. While online blackjack tables and virtual slot machines may grab some of the winnings that would otherwise go to traditional U.S. casinos, various factors, such as the remoteness of betting through a personal computer and concerns about legality, security, and obtaining winnings, will make this form of gambling a less formidable competitor.

The largest supplier of slot machines is International Game Technology, which holds a 72% share of the U.S. market and 74% of the machines in its home state of Nevada. Although IGT fell behind in developing flashy new video slot machines, it has developed close relationships with casinos through its accounting software that keeps record of the money that is won and lost on each slot machine. Close rival, WMS Industries recently filed a lawsuit against IGT, accusing the company of giving away accounting software in exchange for the casino's promise to buy at least 75% of its games from IGT.

Complete the information below and identify the intensity of each of the forces of competition:

1. Rivalry Among Existing Firms   **High   Medium   Low**

    a) Define the gaming industry.

    _____

    _____

    _____

    _____

    _____

    _____

    _____

    _____

    _____

    _____

    _____

b)   What is its level of concentration?

_____

_____

_____

_____

_____

_____

_____

_____

_____

_____

_____

2. Bargaining Power of Suppliers   **High   Medium   Low**

    a) Who are the suppliers?

_____

_____

_____

_____

_____

_____

_____

_____

_____

_____

_____

_____

b) Discuss bargaining power.

_____

_____

_____

_____

_____

_____

_____

_____

_____

_____

_____

3. Bargaining Power of Buyers   **High   Medium   Low**

   a)   Who are the buyers?

_____

_____

_____

_____

_____

_____

_____

_____

_____

_____

_____

b) Discuss whether they have bargaining power.

_____

_____

_____

_____

_____

_____

_____

_____

_____

_____

_____

_____

4. Relative Power of Other Stakeholders   **High   Medium   Low**

   Who are other major stakeholders?

   _____

   _____

   _____

   _____

   _____

   _____

   _____

   _____

   _____

   _____

   _____

   _____

5. Threat of New Entrants   **High   Medium   Low**

    What are the barriers to entry into this industry?

_____

_____

_____

_____

_____

_____

_____

_____

_____

_____

_____

_____

6. Threat of Substitutes   **High   Medium   Low**

What other substitutes limit the sales and profits for firms in this industry?

_____

_____

_____

_____

_____

_____

_____

_____

_____

_____

_____

7. Now that you have analyzed each of the forces of competition, discuss the implications of the above levels of intensity.

   a) Which forces of competition are most threatening now? Which do you expect will change over the next, say, five years?

   _____

   _____

   _____

   _____

   _____

   _____

   _____

   _____

   _____

   _____

   _____

b)   What are the implications in terms of profit margins in this industry today? Over the next
     five years?

_____

_____

_____

_____

_____

_____

_____

_____

_____

_____

_____

_____

c) As the CEO of a firm in this industry, what actions does this analysis suggest you implement in order to strengthen your competitive strategy?

_____

_____

_____

_____

_____

_____

_____

_____

_____

_____

_____

_____

_____

_____

_____

_____

_____

_____

_____

d) As an advisor to a potential entrant, would you recommend entry? What steps would you advise them to take?

_____

_____

_____

_____

_____

_____

Strategy Session 7

Generating a Plan of Action: SWOT Analysis

OBJECTIVE

The SWOT model helps to develop a comprehensive view of the firm in relation to its environment. After reading the introduction, build a plan of action using the SWOT approach to analysis in the exercise that follows.

The term SWOT is one of the most widely used and well known in the field of strategic management. It is an acronym for **S**trengths, **W**eaknesses, **O**pportunities, and **T**hreats, and represents a helpful tool for generating a summary of a strategic situation. Strengths and weaknesses capture the internal environment of the firm and may include skills, expertise, organizational resources, competitive capabilities, positional advantages or disadvantages, market share, brand recognition, or distribution capabilities, to name a few. Opportunities and threats stem from the situation in a company's external competitive environment. The exit of a competitor may, for example, be an opportunity. Or, that society is increasingly concerned about convenience may be a favorable trend for a company whose products and services are designed for busy consumers. New regulations or the emergence of lower-cost technologies, on the other hand, may pose threats.

> *The strategic alternative, which results from matching opportunity and corporate capability at an acceptable level of risk, is what we may call an economic strategy.*
>
> —Kenneth R. Andrews, The Concept of Corporate Strategy

The purpose of this classification was to ensure a good fit between the firm's material, technical, financial, and managerial resources to ensure full exploitation of opportunities while minimizing risks facing the firm.

By putting the four categories in a matrix format (shown in the following exercise), we get a useful tool to generate alternatives in a systematic manner. This enables one to match the elements of strengths and weaknesses with the opportunities and threats. When S and O are matched in the SO box, they represent possible ways in which the organization can use its strengths to take advantage of opportunities and favorable trends in the environment. Similarly, the ST box represents ways in which strengths could be used to protect the organization from threats. The WO suggests areas internally that need to be tackled to take advantage of the opportunities, and WT shows how the weaknesses make the organization most vulnerable against threats and thereby point to defensive tactics.

Once the boxes are completed, some of the entries that represent individual action steps could be combined to show an "alternative" or a set of decisions and actions that represent the future strategy of the organization. An additional step is to list the actions in a decreasing order of importance for the organization or and to differentiate those that deal with the long term as against the short term.

As used in the field of strategic management, the SWOT approach goes beyond being a list of items under four categories. The number of items does not matter. What is important is that they be stated in a specific manner. For instance, rather than saying "Good marketing skills," it is better to specify what aspect of marketing a company can do well. Or, instead of listing "International expansion" as an opportunity, try to narrow it down further by specifying country or region, for which particular products, and so on. Moreover, it is not just matching strengths with opportunities that is important. Consideration of weaknesses and threats is also crucial in the matching process. The intersection of weaknesses and threats represent areas where the organization is particularly vulnerable, especially in a very competitive environment. Steps the organization could take to mitigate potential threats and strengthen its position are important components of an action plan.

 Strategy_Online

The Strategic Perspectives Web site provides another view of SWOT:

www.strategic-p.com

And an example of SWOT analysis applied to the dairy industry in India is available at the Indian Dairy Industry Web site:

www.indiadairy.com/ind_swot.html

Exercise: An Action Plan for Robin Hood

INSTRUCTIONS

Read the "Robin Hood" case below. Look at Robin Hood and his band of Merrymen as an organization.

1. Identify elements of their organizational strengths and weaknesses. Examine the external environment and identify opportunities and threats they face. Enter the items identified in the appropriate places in the chart in Figure 7.1 that follows the case.

2. Next, one by one, match the elements from the 'Internal' axis (S or W) with ones from the 'External' axis (O or T) and write them as an action steps in the inside boxes labeled SO, WO, ST, and WT. A brief example is given in the chart in Figure 7.1 to illustrate the process. Then answer questions 1 and 2 that follow.

ROBIN HOOD

It was in the spring of the second year of his insurrection against the High Sheriff of Nottingham that Robin Hood took a walk in Sherwood Forest. As he walked, he pondered the progress of the campaign, the disposition of his forces, the Sheriff's recent moves, and the options that confronted him.

The revolt against the Sheriff had begun as a personal crusade. It erupted out of Robin's conflict with the Sheriff and his administration. However, alone Robin Hood could do little. He therefore sought allies, men with grievances and a deep sense of justice. Later he welcomed all who came, asking few questions and demanding only a willingness to serve. Strength, he believed, lay in numbers.

He spent the first year forging the group into a disciplined band, united in enmity against the Sheriff and willing to live outside the law. The band's organization was simple. Robin ruled supreme, making all-important decisions. He delegated specific tasks to his lieutenants. Will Scarlett was in charge of intelligence and scouting. His main job was to shadow the Sheriff and his men, always alert to their next move. He also collected information on the travel plans of rich merchants and tax collectors. Little John kept discipline among the men, and saw to it that their archery was at the high peak that their profession demanded. Scarlock took care of the finances, converting loot to cash, paying shares of the take, and finding suitable hiding places for the surplus. Finally, Much, the Miller's son, had the difficult task of provisioning the ever-increasing band of Merrymen.

The increasing size of the band was a source of satisfaction for Robin, but also a source of concern. The fame of his Merrymen was spreading, and new recruits poured in from every corner of England. As the band grew larger, their small bivouac became a major encampment. Between raids the men milled about, talking and playing games. Vigilance declined, and discipline was becoming harder to enforce. "Why," Robin reflected, "I don't know half the men I run into these days."

The growing band was also beginning to exceed the food capacity of the forest. Game was becoming scarce, and supplies had to be obtained from outlying villages. The cost of buying food was beginning to drain the band's financial reserves at the very moment when revenues were in decline. Travelers, especially those with the most to lose, were now giving the forest a wide berth. This was costly and inconvenient to them, but it was preferable to having all their goods confiscated.

Robin believed that the time had come for the Merrymen to change their policy of outright confiscation of goods to one of a fixed transit tax. His lieutenants strongly resisted this idea. They were proud of the Merrymen's famous motto "Rob from the rich and give to the poor." "The farmers and the townspeople," they argued, "are our most important allies. How can we tax them, and still hope for their help in our fight against the Sheriff?"

Robin wondered how long the Merrymen could keep to the ways and methods of their early days. The Sheriff was growing stronger and becoming better organized. He now had the money and the men and was beginning to harass the band, probing for its weaknesses. The tide of events was beginning to turn against the Merrymen. Robin felt that the campaign must be decisively concluded before the Sheriff had a chance to deliver a mortal blow. "But how," he wondered, "could this be done?"

Robin had often entertained the possibility of killing the Sheriff, but the chances for this seemed increasingly remote. Besides, killing the Sheriff might satisfy his personal thirst for revenge, but it would not improve the situation. Robin had hoped that the perpetual state of unrest, and the Sheriff's failure to collect taxes, would lead to his removal from office. Instead, the Sheriff used his political connections to obtain reinforcement. He had powerful friends at court and was well regarded by the regent, Prince John.

Prince John was vicious and volatile. He was consumed by his unpopularity among the people, who wanted the imprisoned King Richard back. He also lived in constant fear of the barons, who had first given him the regency, but were now beginning to dispute his claim to the throne. Several of these barons had set out to collect the ransom that would release King Richard the Lionheart from his jail in Austria. Robin was invited to join the conspiracy in return for future amnesty. It was a dangerous proposition. Provincial banditry was one thing, court intrigue another. Prince John had spies everywhere, and he was known for his vindictiveness. If the conspirators' plan failed, the pursuit would be relentless, and retributions swift.

The sound of the supper horn startled Robin from his thoughts. There was the smell of roasting venison in the air. Nothing was resolved or settled. Robin headed for camp promising himself that he would give these problems his utmost attention after tomorrow's raid.

Figure 7.1   SWOT Analysis Chart for "Robin Hood"

INTERNAL

	Strengths Size: more fighting men	**Weaknesses**
Opportunities **(Favorable Trends)** 1. Other forests available	**SO** 1. Expand operations to other forests (S1,O1)	**WO**
Threats **(Unfavorable Trends)** 1. Game (food) becoming scarce	**ST** 1. Create separate group with a different mission—to hunt for food and not involved in robbing. (S1,T1)	**WT**

EXTERNAL

1. The boxes SO, WO, ST and WT contain individual action steps. Some could be combined to generate two or more alternative courses of action. List the alternatives below.

_____

_____

_____

_____

_____

_____

_____

_____

_____

_____

_____

_____

_____

_____

_____

_____

2. What criteria will you use to choose the action steps to follow?

_____

_____

_____

_____

_____

_____

_____

_____

Strategy Session 8

Developing Generic Strategy

OBJECTIVE

In this session, consider the advantages of generic strategy and then compare organizations in the exercise—ones that pursue each of the four kinds of generic strategies—and a firm that is stuck in the middle.

Organizations develop a business-level strategy by using company resources and distinctive competencies to gain a competitive advantage over rivals in an industry. Michael Porter, who developed the framework for business-level strategy, labeled it *generic strategy* because in principle, the choices of strategy can be applied to any business and any industry.

Generic strategy choices involve two dimensions: competitive advantage and competitive scope. In seeking the competitive advantage, a company might choose a low cost strategy when trying to outperform other firms in a particular industry. This strategy is the ability of a company to design, produce, and market a product more efficiently and at a lower cost than its competitors. Alternatively, a company might choose a differentiation strategy as a means of gaining competitive advantage. Differentiation is the ability to provide products or services that are perceived to be unique by customers and for which they are willing to pay more. For example, Maytag produces washers and other household appliances that consumers pay more for because they are advertised to be of better quality and rarely need service.

A manufacturer should and must excel all competition in some way . . . the product can be more efficiently made and be cheaper in price . . . or designed for different uses. Or it may be applied to the customer's needs in a way that will make it more useful because of the application.

—James F. Lincoln

Besides competitive advantage, a firm must choose its competitive scope, either targeting a broad market or a narrow—or niche—market. A broad market scope implies that the firm targets the mass market or many market segments, whereas the narrow market scope focuses on one particular buyer group.

Combining the two types of competitive advantage with the two types of target markets results in four potential variations of generic strategy options. When the lower cost and differentiation strategies of a broad mass-market target, they are referred to as *cost leadership* and *differentiation*. When they are targeting only one buyer group, they are called *focus cost leadership* and *focus differentiation*.

According to Porter, the greatest danger in pursuing a generic strategy is the possibility of being stuck in the middle. From a competitive advantage standpoint, this occurs when a firm is unwilling to commit marketing and research-and-development resources needed to create a product or service that is perceived to be unique, or when a firm tries to keep costs low but does not aggressively pursue strategies to have the lowest cost in the industry. Regarding competitive scope, a firm that is pursuing a focus strategy can be stuck in the middle when it becomes overconfident and starts to go after many market segments or expand into the mass market without committing the necessary resources to successfully reach the larger market.

Although some companies appear to achieve both a low-cost and a high-differentiation position, Porter argues that this state is often temporary. In order to achieve above average profits over the long run, a firm must commit resources to one specific competitive strategy.

Strategy_Online

Read the CEO's views about how Maytag differentiates products in all of its divisions. Navigate your browser to the Maytag Corporation Web site address shown below. Click the "Inside Maytag" hyperlink in the navigation bar, and then click "From the CEO" to read Lloyd D. Ward's statement:

www.Maytagcorp.com

Exercise: Choosing How to Compete in the Lodging Industry

INSTRUCTIONS

Read the lodging industry profile located in Part IV (pp. 147–152). On an individual basis, identify features and descriptive characteristics for five hypothetical companies in Table 8.1 on the following page. The information from the lodging industry profile provides background information about the industry and environmental trends.

TEAM ACTIVITY: TOP MANAGEMENT TEAM

INSTRUCTIONS

You are the top management team who is proposing a new hotel entering the lodging industry. You will be assigned Company A, B, C, D, or E by your instructor. Prepare a poster depicting the type of hotel you will build using the guidelines below and be sure to follow the strategy that has been assigned to your company. The poster will be used to sell the idea of the hotel and the organization to potential investors who might want to fund the company as it attempts to capture its target market. When you are finished, put your poster on the wall and choose one member of your group to "sell" your hotel and your organization. You have 45 minutes to complete this exercise.

Be prepared to discuss how your strategy will take advantage of environmental trends.

Guidelines for Preparing the Team Poster and Presentation

1. What kind of hotel would you build? What would it be called? Describe its five main features.

2. How would you market your hotel? To whom?

3. Describe three specific skills or resources you would use. How would you use them?

4. Describe two features of the organization (structure, incentive systems, etc.).

Table 8.1 Identifying the Characteristics of the Four Kinds of Generic Strategies

Strategy	Company Features and Description	Target Market	Environmental Trends That Support Strategy	Environmental Trends That Threaten Strategy
Stuck in the middle: Company E				
Focus differentiator: Company D				
Focus cost leadership: Company C				
Differentiator: Company B				
Cost leadership: Company A				

Strategy Session 9

Viewing Corporate Strategy from the Core Competencies Perspective

OBJECTIVE

In this session, practice designing corporate strategy for a diversified company from a core competencies perspective.

Corporate strategy deals with making choices about the direction for a firm as a whole and about the areas in which a company should compete. In choosing business areas, management decides whether to concentrate resources and create competitive advantage in one line of business or in one industry, such as McDonald's in the fast-food industry and Delta Airlines in the airline industry, or to select and manage a mix of businesses competing in several industries, such as General Electric and Johnson & Johnson. Either way, issues of growth or downsizing become part of what is considered corporate-level strategic decision making.

Since the 1960s, U.S. companies in particular followed corporate strategies of growth by expanding product offerings and diversifying into different business areas. To help executives make decisions about how to divide organizational resources and where to invest new capital, several portfolio models were created. Among the most well known were the BCG growth/share matrix, the GE/McKinsey industry attractiveness and business strength model, and the Arthur D. Little matrix that incorporated life-cycle stages into the analysis. These techniques provided a convenient

If we build a new attraction, we feature it in our magazines, on the Disney channels, in a trailer in front of Disney movies, in the windows of our retail stores, on consumer products, and Disney Records promotes the music. There is not a single part of Disney where the left hand can't wash the right.

—Michael Eisner, Chairman & CEO of Disney

means for management to review the competitive position of diversified business units against one another all on one chart.

While these models simplified large amounts of information about a multidivisional firm's many holdings, the "portfolio of businesses" approach had limitations. It focused on viewing businesses in the portfolio as freestanding units, an approach that could fragment and misguide resource allocation. For example, pulling resources from a strong business unit that operated in a low-growth mature industry to fund an up-and-coming unit in a high-growth industry could actually result in the premature decline of the strong unit. Also, this approach gave little guidance to management in terms of what new businesses should be added to the company's holdings and how to increase overall revenues.

To promote a wider view of the firm beyond a collection of individual business units, Hamel and Prahalad created a framework that considers the firm as a portfolio of core competencies. The idea of core competencies in business comes from the resource-based view of strategic thinking. This view holds that strategy should be developed based on a company's unique resources and capabilities. Resources include capital equipment, the skills of employees, patents, finance, and talented managers. Capabilities are the skills needed to take full advantage of a firm's assets. Competitive advantage occurs when resources and capabilities are

- Valuable to a company's chosen direction
- Rare
- Costly to imitate
- Cannot easily be substituted

When these four criteria are met, resources and capabilities become core competencies (see Figure 9.1).

Figure 9.1   Core Competencies

Resources and Capabilities that are valuable, rare, costly to imitate, nonsubstitutable = **Core Competencies**

By viewing the firm as a portfolio of core competencies rather than as a collection of individual business units, management is in a better position to identify acquisition and deployment goals. That is, it focuses attention on how a company can create value by building new competencies or by recombining existing competencies to enter new business areas.

To actively manage core competencies, managers must share a view of what those core competencies are. While many managers can articulate what is done well in the organization, it may be more difficult for them to separate competencies from the products or services offered. For example, at Canon, the core competencies are not their color copiers or bubble jet printers. Rather, their capability for precision mechanics, fine optics, and electronic imaging that result in the end products. Therefore, the first step in creating this type of portfolio is to identify an inventory of competencies separate from the inventory of products or services.

The matrix below shows these two dimensions (core competencies and product-markets) at two time frames: existing and new. The inventory discussed above of existing competencies and existing product-markets falls in the lower left quadrant of the matrix. Once the inventory is prepared, management is ready to move to the next step of considering strategic options. Are there opportunities to strengthen the company's position in a particular product area by importing competencies that may exist elsewhere in the company? This was a strategy adopted by General Electric when it transferred competencies between its power generator business and its jet engine business, both of which rely on advanced materials and engineering skills to produce large turbines.

Other strategic options involve considering new core competencies and new product-markets (see Figure 9.2). The advantage of this framework is that it seeks to identify and exploit the interlinkages across units. Whether management chooses to diversify into related or unrelated industries or whether the company remains in one industry and competencies are shared across product lines, this technique keeps management focused on adding value to the corporate whole from a resource-based, core competencies' perspective.

Figure 9.2   New Core Competencies and New Product-markets

		Existing	New
Core Competencies	**New**	What new core competencies are needed to protect and extend existing markets?	What new core competencies would we need to participate in new markets?
	Existing	This is the existing portfolio or inventory of competencies and products. What is the opportunity to improve the company's position in existing markets through existing core competencies?	What new products or services could be created through recombining current core competencies?
		Existing	**New**
		Product-Markets	

   Strategy_Online

The Tuck School of Business at Dartmouth University publishes Strategy+Business *online magazine, which features excellent articles, archives and works-in-progress on the issues examined in this course:*

www.strategy-business.com

Exercise: Corporate Strategy at Walt Disney Company

INSTRUCTIONS

Read and use the Walt Disney Company profile below to complete the Table 9.1 at the end of the exercise as part of a team activity.

WALT DISNEY COMPANY

In the early 1920s, Walt Disney saw the potential for developing quality animated cartoons for the motion picture industry; and he and his brother Roy started the Walt Disney Bros. Studio. With the skill of creative animation, the company developed the still famous characters of Mickey Mouse, Donald Duck, Goofy, and other characters. By combining technical developments with a popular and emerging cast of cartoon characters, Disney developed a distinctive strength that no competitors could match. Other studios created animation departments, but none could match the renamed Walt Disney Production Company's technological innovation and popular characters.

Walt Disney expanded production beyond movie shorts to full-length cartoon motion pictures, the first being *Snow White and the Seven Dwarves* (1937). In the 1950s, Disney realized that animation was not the only way to bring the public's favorite fantasy characters to the screen, and the studios produced movies such as *Treasure Island* and *The Swiss Family Robinson*. Disney continued to produce animation movies with hits such a *101 Dalmatians* and *Peter Pan*. By 1960, experiments with combining animation and live action resulted in the release of *Mary Poppins,* one of the all-time hits for Disney.

With a mission of providing fun and fantasy to the public, Disney moved into television with the Mickey Mouse Club and other programming. Television also enabled the company to promote Walt Disney's dream of a theme park. The combination of theme park (which Disney saw as of exploiting the popularity of his Disney characters and of bringing the family a fun-filled day of Disney fantasy), television, and movies fed on and promoted each other.

After Disney's death in 1966 and until 1984, the company's creative mission lacked its founder's direction. Profits from the theme parks and moviemaking declined, and the Disney Channel that came on line in 1983 had huge startup costs that drained the company. One bright spot in that year was the sale Disney classics on videocassette. Disney's licensing arm, which licensed characters, songs, and music to various manufacturers, retailers, and publishers, generated revenue; but for every dollar it collected, Disney product licensees earned five times that amount.

The Eisner era   When Michael Eisner became CEO of Disney in 1984, his strategy was to develop existing units and to aggressively pursue growth into new areas of business for Disney . The noncore growth was so successful that at the end of 1995, the majority of growth Eisner achieved was from new business development and acquisitions that did not exist before his appointment. These included international film distribution, television broadcasting, newspaper, magazine, and book publishing, the Disney Stores, live theatrical entertainment, ownership of professional sport teams, online computer programs, Disney Cruise Line, and home video production. Revenues for 1995 reached a record $12.11 billion with operating income hitting an all-time high of $2.45 billion. In 1999, Disney merged its Internet assets with Infoseek Corp., creating a new tracking stock called Go.com. The new stock will track the performance of Disney's Internet properties and the Infoseek assets.

Disney's recent performance   By the end of 1999, Disney was a large corporate entertainment company. It had seven theme parks (and four more in development), 27 hotels with 36,888 rooms, two cruise ships, 728 Disney Stores, one broadcast network, 10 TV stations, nine international Disney Channels, 42 radio stations, an Internet portal, five major Internet web sites, and interests in nine U.S. cable networks. The company enhanced its film library with 17 animated films, 265 live-action films, 1,252 animated television episodes, and 6,505 live-action television episodes.

However, financial performance no longer improved as the company grew. The decline began in 1996 when earnings were lower than the previous year, a first in the Eisner era. Performance continued to level off for the next two years, and analysts suggested that the company's $19 billion acquisition of Capital Cities/ABC, Inc. had placed a strain on its future growth potential. ABC's ratings lagged behind other networks, and its ad revenues were falling. Eisner promised a turnaround by 2001. For the first quarter of 2000, the success of "Who Wants to be a Millionaire?," an ABC runaway hit, boosted Disney's bottom line by $100 million. Still, the consumer products division, which includes The Disney Stores, Disney Interactive, and Disney Online, had not met performance expectations. In particular, The Disney Store chain struggled with outdated goods and overcrowded aisles. The company has pursued a drive to pare down or dispose of noncore operations, a drive that began in 1998 with the sale of its Fairchild Publications unit. Disney also explored the sale of its baseball and hockey teams.

Eisner promises to get back into day-to-day operations, particularly in movie production, theme park rides, and Disney Store redesign as a result of the recent appointment of Robert Iger as president and chief operating officer and Peter Murphy as strategic planning chief. The question remains whether the company's strategies for the four major divisions (see Table 9.1) will achieve the promised turnaround by 2001 and whether the company's core skills have created synergies among the divisions.

Table 9.1   Company Strategy for Disney's Four Major Divisions of Disney

Division	1999 Revenue	1999 Operating Income	Strategy
Media networks	$7.5 billion	$1.6 billion	Ride success of ABC programs and raise rates on cable channels
Studio entertainment	6.5 billion	116 million	Cut back on big-budget films, restructure home video
Theme parks and resorts	6.1 billion	1.4 billion	Drive profits with new California park
Consumer products	3.0 billion	607 million	Cut back on licensees, remodel Disney Stores

TEAM ACTIVITY: RATING THE DISNEY COMPANY

Names: _____

_____

1. As a team, complete the information for the Disney Company in the boxes on this page and the next.

	Core Competencies	Product-markets
1923–1983		

	Core Competencies	Product-markets
1984–2000		

2. As of the year 2000, using the scale below, rate how well you think the company has linked its core competencies to new product-markets:

Rating = _____

5 = Linkage is the strongest that it has been in the company's history.

4 = Linkage is improving as a result of new product-markets (during the Eisner era).

3 = Linkage is the same before and during the Eisner era.

2 = Link is getting weaker as a result of new product-markets (during the Eisner era).

1 = No linkage between core competencies and product-markets exists.

Strategy Session 10

Global Strategic Alliances

OBJECTIVE

In this session, the goal is to understand the nature of a strategic alliance between companies and the decisions required to make it work. After completing this introductory reading, complete the exercise about the General Motors-Toyota alliance that follows.

A strategic alliance may be defined very broadly as any arrangement or agreement under which two or more firms cooperate to achieve certain commercial objectives. Given this definition, the term covers a wide range of options, from simple agreements to buy and sell each other's goods, to creating separate and legally distinct ventures. Although the objectives of an alliance can vary widely, if properly dealt with, an alliance can be a relatively inexpensive way of achieving targeted objectives.

Game theory and transaction cost analysis are two theories that help explain why firms might consider creating a strategic alliance. Game theory suggests that firms will cooperate rather than compete when benefits are maximized. Transaction cost analysis, on the other hand, would suggest ownership of resources is more efficient than contracting for goods and services when the transaction cost of buying goods on the open market becomes too great.

First, according to game theory, the alliance can be seen as an example of how cooperation can maximize benefits for the two partners. The need for careful structuring of cooperation arises since the notion of an alliance suffers from some inherent contradictions, especially when it involves two players in the same or related industry. The contradictions occur because there are often positive and defensive objectives associated with the alliance, even though the two partners will not enter into an alliance unless they hope to gain more from cooperating than being on their own. On the positive side, the objectives for each partner are to add value to the activity on which they are cooperating and to enhance their competencies through learning from the partner. On the defensive side is the need to avoid becoming very dependent on the partner, which would reduce the other firm's flexibility in strategic decision making and to ensure that its core competencies are not being absorbed and learned by the partner. The latter, in particular, may make the firm less attractive and reduce its competitive edge.

From the game theory perspective, one can argue that the very concept of an alliance consists of factors that can cause tension and lead to failure. Thus, there is a need for careful structuring of the alliance. Before entering into an agreement, the parties must carefully select each other, be clear about their objectives, bring complementary strengths to the alliance, and ensure the benefits to cooperation are maximized. Sometimes entering into long-term commitments can help achieve these benefits.

> *In the fluid global marketplace, it is no longer possible or desirable for single organizations to be entirely self-sufficient. Collaboration is the value of the future. Alliances are the structure of the future*
>
> —Joel Bleeke and David Ernst

The second theory that helps to explain the need for an alliance is transaction cost analysis. This theory suggests that an alliance should deliver greater benefits to the two parties than what might be achieved from a purely market based transaction between them or with others for similar goods and services. That is, if the two parties can achieve their objectives through outsourcing their needs, or outright purchase of components, there is no need to enter into an alliance. As a result, this approach calls for detailed contractual agreements between the parties that clearly cover the cost-benefit issues; and as trust develops, the costs can be reduced with less supervision and better interaction between the partners.

Whether an alliance is created because cooperation offers greater benefits or because transaction costs can be reduced, parties go through in forming an alliance three important stages. These are (1) the careful selection of a partner, (2) negotiation and structuring of the agreement, and (3) the post-agreement management of the alliance. In addition, several features contribute to a successful alliance:

1. The partnership should preferably be between "equals." When partners bring complementary skills and keep their objectives clear, there is less room for confusion.
2. An ownership interest and clearly stated contractual rights and obligations help cement and deepen commitment to the alliance.
3. Partners should recognize differences in management styles and cultures and work towards dealing with these issues openly and in a sensitive manner.
4. Regular review of progress in the alliance keeps a focus on objectives and prevents problems from getting too large before they are sorted out.

 Strategy_Online

For exploring alliances and how companies use them, visit the Web site of banking firm of Fredericks Michael & Company, click the Advisory Services hyperlink, and then choose the Strategic Alliances link:

www.fm-co.com

You should also visit the Web site of Cisco Systems, the computer-networking giant. Several of its alliances are discussed in the following Web page:

www.cisco.com/warp/public/756/partnership/

Exercise: Making the General Motors-Toyota Alliance Work

INSTRUCTIONS

Read the case "General Motors-Toyota Alliance" below and complete the first question in the form that follows before coming to class. Then, in class, the instructor will have you form into teams and provide you with updated information and instructions for the next step of this exercise.

NUMMI: THE GENERAL MOTORS-TOYOTA ALLIANCE

In 1983, General Motors (GM) and Toyota entered into an alliance that resulted in the creation of the New United Motor Manufacturing Incorporated (NUMMI), a new company that would be equally owned by the two parents and with equal representation on the board of directors. Toyota's contribution to NUMMI was $100 million in cash. GM also contributed the same amount, made up of $20 million in cash and its plant in Freemont, California, which would be the NUMMI manufacturing facility.

GM had two objectives for the alliance with Toyota. One was to gain quick access to a world-class small car, a gap in GM's product line that could be filled by Toyota's perceived strengths in this area. The other was to learn about Toyota's famous production system. This system was credited with having achieved very low inventory levels and high efficiency. GM's plant in Freemont, California, had been idle for a year. Started in 1963, it had been shut down and its workers laid off due to poor labor-management relations, high absenteeism, and the alcohol-related problems of employees affecting operations.

Toyota had intentions of being in the North American market for the long term. However, it was unaware of how to deal with the United Auto Workers (the labor union in the auto industry) and U.S. suppliers. A manufacturing presence in the U.S. was important for its long-term goals, and the company hoped that an alliance with GM would help it learn how to work with these groups.

Under the terms of the alliance, Toyota would appoint the president, CEO, and NUMMI's other top officers. GM would assign a maximum of 16 executives on three-year assignments on a rotating basis. NUMMI would be a stamping and assembly operation, and components would be supplied both from Japan (by Toyota) and other suppliers in the U.S. The initial product was a compact car that Toyota had already been making and selling in Japan. It was called the Chevy Nova and sold for about $7,500. Toyota agreed to GM's condition (not included in the contract) that the laid-off UAW workers would be employed in the plant.

In managing NUMMI, Toyota followed many of its established practices, such as carefully selecting employees, training workers for more than one job and delegating decision making to small worker teams. Thousands of GM employees took tours of the facility, and the company created a liaison office in California to document what it was learning about the production system at NUMMI. The team approach was transferred to GM plants in New Jersey and Delaware. Over time, GM agreed to job security conditions and limits on plant closings in contracts with the UAW, conditions that were not normally part of GM and the UAW contracts. In 1987, GM went so far as to set up committees of workers and managers in every one of the company's plants to find ways to improve productivity and quality. Nonetheless, the type of labor-management cooperation that existed at NUMMI did not occur at all GM plants. For example, at the company's facility in Van Nuys, California, differences in how the company approached the issue of trust in dealing with the union continued to hamper labor-management cooperation.

As of 1998, NUMMI employed about 4,800 workers. The plant has maintained high quality and high productivity standards. The production rate achieved is about 60 cars per hour using only about one-third of the workers in a comparable auto plant elsewhere. Some workers' representatives complained about this fast pace, as reported in the press, yet they still participate in ongoing learning and continuous improvement. The company is credited with having established a problem-solving approach in its relationship with the same union that formerly fought GM's management. Absenteeism has dropped from 22% to 2%. Toyota continues to manage the factory and produces three vehicles: Toyota Tacoma pickup trucks, Toyota Corolla sedans, and Geo Prizms.

Although NUMMI produces cars for both GM and Toyota, marketing is the responsibility of the respective parent. The alliance partners market the same car produced on the assembly line with different brand names, and the car has very different market perceptions associated not with the unit but with the parent. For instance, if the car is marketed by Toyota as a *Corolla FX*, it is sold with ease and without financial incentives. However, the same car marketed as a *Prizm* by GM requires several incentives. Even eight years after launch, consumers ask whether these are really the same car.

The Toyota-GM collaboration has extended to other areas. Toyota recently expanded its purchase of computer accessories from GM for its production lines in Japan. Toyota also sells Chevrolet Cavaliers under its brand name in Japan, and the two companies have worked together on inductive charging systems for electric vehicles. The companies said the impetus for collaborating was the high cost and risk inherent in developing untested alternative technologies to replace the internal-combustion engine.

A new five-year partnership announced in April 1999 aims to develop and possibly jointly produce advanced-technology vehicles, including those powered by fuel cells. GM is today the world's No. 1 automaker, and Toyota, No. 3 worldwide. Together, they account for 25% of global auto production.

In spite of these collaborations, the two companies exhibit other normal competitive conditions. In 1998, Toyota recruited a manager with experience in pickup truck production from GM to head the production function in its new manufacturing plant in Princeton, Indiana. All trucks sold in the U.S. have been by the three U.S. automakers, and Toyota hopes to challenge their supremacy in this area with its own new truck, the *Tundra*. Incidentally, the manager, Mr. Norm Bafunno, had done a stint earlier at NUMMI and transferred the knowledge he gained when he returned to GM production. Bafunno now says that although the famed Toyota production system is not unique anymore, since more and more manufacturers have learned and adopted it in their own factories, he still sees several differences in the way Toyota runs its production. The rules focus on the factory workers, giving them the power to make improvements in production, eliminate waste, and make quality judgments about the product.

Alliances are not new to GM. The company has an alliance with Isuzu, which involves financing arrangements, product development, and even joint ownership of manufacturing plants around the world. In addition, GM has alliances in automobiles with Daewoo in Korea, with Hitachi (electronics), Fanuc (robots), and many others. The alliances have spanned the range of contractual arrangements, minority equity participation, and joint ventures. Industry observers have a very mixed opinion about GM's experience. There are some who think these are ad hoc solutions undertaken by GM without any lasting impact on the organization and from which the firm may benefit, if any, only in the short term. There are others, however, who believe that GM has adopted a new form of a competitive organization, which will make a lasting impact on the company's policies and performance.

Some observers feel that GM has not really learned the inherent nature of the Toyota system, only the structure. For example, GM believes there is one "best way" to produce a car. Toyota, however, approaches production very differently. Its leaner system is more than just *kanban* (a just-in-time production system where parts arrive just in time for manufacture) and where productivity and quality are maintained at high levels. Instead, it is a broad system, which engages its participants in their work with an ideology that appeals to their hearts and minds. As Haruo Shimada of Japan's Keio University has said, the Toyota system amounts to "humanware": combining management, participation, incentives, and technology to optimize productivity, motivation, and the development of people at work.

Toyota's ideology is reflected at NUMMI in many ways. NUMMI has robots that are designed to make people's jobs easier. For example, robots do heavy lifting and are not intended primarily as labor- or cost-saving devices. The idea is that technology should be a tool and that workers should add wisdom to the machines. Moreover, the company stresses the importance of leadership at every level to create trust and facilitate learning.

Many U.S. manufacturers that have adopted the Toyota system miss the mark and do not focus on how Toyota eliminates inventory, defects, and waste. Also, at NUMMI, workers who teach and help others are promoted to team leadership roles. At Toyota's Japanese factories, supervisors are even given a budget to entertain workers periodically, buy them a beer, and strengthen relationships within teams. This contrasts with GM's traditional plants even today, where supervisors are upset with workers when they try to prevent defects by stopping the assembly line.

Based on your reading of the case, complete Question 1.

1. What are the areas of cooperation and conflict that arise from the NUMMI alliance for both companies? Use Table 10.1 to answer this question. Try to separate the issues you would consider strategic and operational for the organization.

Table 10.1   Areas of Cooperation and Conflict

	Cooperation	Conflict
Strategic		
Operational		

TEAM ACTIVITY: NEGOTIATIONS

After negotiation in class, answer the following series of questions. Check your team's "company" as appropriate:

☐ **Toyota**   ☐ **GM**

2. What objectives did you have in mind for the renegotiation?

_____

_____

_____

_____

_____

_____

_____

_____

_____

_____

3. What elements in the agreement help in maximizing the benefit for your company?

_____

_____

_____

_____

_____

_____

_____

_____

_____

_____

_____

_____

4. What elements in the agreement have minimized the potential for future conflicts?

_____

_____

_____

_____

_____

_____

_____

_____

_____

_____

_____

_____

5. How would you judge whether NUMMI is a success or not?

_____

_____

_____

_____

_____

_____

_____

_____

_____

_____

_____

Strategy Session 11

Identifying Transnational Strategies

OBJECTIVE

This session develops an understanding of the choices a company has in formulating a transnational strategy and in making it work. The exercise includes company profiles of two global footwear giants: Bata Shoes and Nike.

Due to the trend towards globalization of most sectors of the economy, more organizations today have global strategies that involve them in business operations worldwide. As companies ponder about the strategy they should adopt in different nations, they are faced with the choice of following a common strategy across all the nations or designing a unique one for each country. Should operations and products be standardized or customized? This choice is commonly referred to in the literature as *global versus multidomestic strategy*.

A company following a ***global*** (or standardized) ***strategy*** tends to take a centralized and coordinated view of its strategy across the globe since it believes that the similarities of markets allow for exploiting a common strategy. These companies are highly focused on global profitability and would therefore coordinate activities across the world to maximize the benefits derived from each location and operation. The marketing, R&D, production, and other operational activities of this company may be distributed across the globe or be concentrated in one place depending on scale/scope economies

Lines on a map mean little to a corporation. When a firm is considering where to build a plant, it bases its decisions for the most part on the economic merits of the location, wherever it may be.

—Kenichi Ohmae

and how it fits a global plan. These companies tend to have rather standardized products and thus cater to a customer segment that has generic attributes across countries and is not seeking local responsiveness. This approach is on the rise, as products with worldwide acceptance continue to emerge and as less expensive transportation and communication networks make globalization efficient and effective. One disadvantage of this strategy is that companies may not be able to market to segments that may be looking for something different.

A company that follows a ***multidomestic*** (or customized) ***strategy*** tends to look upon its strategy in each country as being independent of that in another, since it believes that national markets differ significantly in their structure and key success factors. This strategy gives a high preference to location and national considerations. In each individual country, operations would tend to be involved in as many value creation activities as possible, including marketing, production, financing, R&D, and other operational activities. Three social forces encourage customized operations and products. First, cultural differences continue to exist among countries, and different tactics are necessary to target these differences. Second, governments often require that organizations follow legal mandates of the host nation. Third, as competition increases, local firms become aggressive niche players that closely tailor products and services to consumer needs. One disadvantage of this approach is that multinational organizations may not get the benefits of the experience-curve of the company as a whole, as country operations run independent of each other. The Figure 11.1 illustrates these choices on a continuum from standardized to customized strategy.

Figure 11.1   The continuum between global and multidomestic strategies

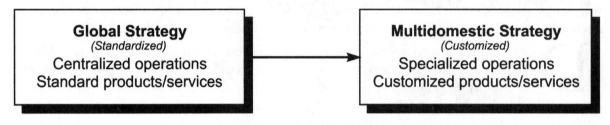

Global Strategy
(Standardized)
Centralized operations
Standard products/services

Multidomestic Strategy
(Customized)
Specialized operations
Customized products/services

    Strategy_Online

For a look at how IKEA, the Swedish furniture and home furnishings manufacturer, has gone global, navigate your Web browser to its corporate site:

www.ikea.com

A profile of the company can also be viewed at:

www.geocities.com/TimesSquare/1848/ikea.html

Exercise: Global Operations of Bata Shoe and Nike

INSTRUCTIONS

Read the company profiles of Bata and Nike. Then respond to the statements that follow, which pertain to different operational areas, by circling a response in the scales below each statement. Then respond, in brief essay form, to Question 10 with your own views.

BATA SHOE ORGANIZATION

The Bata Shoe Organization (BSO) runs the global operations of Bata Ltd. Based in Toronto, Canada, it is credited with being the world's largest manufacturer and retailer of footwear, selling about 350 million pairs a year. (Being family owned, revenue and profit figures are not released.) It operates in 69 countries employing about 52,000 people. It owns 5,000 stores, apart from distributing through over 100,000 retailers and franchisees worldwide. Its 70 manufacturing units worldwide include shoe manufacturing, mold making, quality control laboratories, hosiery units, and tanneries. With a reputation for sturdy, mass-merchandized shoes, it is a well-known name in Africa, Latin America, and Asia. In the U.S., it owns an industrial footwear business.

Tom Bata, Sr., an octogenarian, and the tenth generation of a family of shoemakers, runs the company. The family, originally operating from Czechoslovakia, had built a shoe network in 28 countries by the 1930s and migrated to Canada at the time of the Nazi invasion of the country. Eighty-five percent of its subsidiaries are wholly owned; although in some countries, due to local regulations, Bata Ltd. has only a minority ownership. Where it has no equity, it provides licensing, consulting and technical assistance. BSO keeps a watchful eye over its autonomous subsidiaries. For instance, Bata India, which is 51% owned by Bata Ltd., had a record loss of $9.8 million in 1995. The unit had moved away from its mainstay, the low- to medium-priced shoes, and had been aiming at the high-end footwear market. BSO intervened by sending expatriate managers with turnaround experience, providing fresh investments and an interest free loan of $10 million. By 1997, Bata India had begun on a path of recovery.

Bata's strategy is to provide footwear at affordable prices to the largest possible segment of the population. Factories and stores are built to a standard specification around the world. Bata focuses on low cost manufacturing and builds a local network of retailers and suppliers around it. It takes advantage of local materials in the countries where its plants are based. It prefers to produce in a given market nearly everything it sells there and does not undertake any significant exports and imports between countries.

The company operates in several low-income countries and is conscious of its role as a provider of jobs in the economy. While top management may be composed of expatriates, local personnel are inducted, trained, and given increasing responsibilities. Regular training programs are conducted at Toronto for worldwide employees. Country based training programs work towards solutions to local problems that are culture-sensitive to their area.

BSO deals with a variety of political environments and has units in democratic and totalitarian regimes. In some countries, their operations have been nationalized and then denationalized. It sponsors sporting events and contributes to local causes. The corporate brochure describes the firm as "an international organization of companies rooted in their communities and essentially 'national' in spirit."

Many of the company's factories are located away from urban centers. Bata provides houses, schools, and other amenities for its workers. In some countries, tariff protection and other government incentives have helped protect its market. The coming of manufacturers like Nike and Reebok, however, into the industry on a global scale caused changes in consumer preferences. Innovation and brand image in the footwear industry in the early 1990s caused the industry to be more market rather than manufacturing driven.

Tom Bata Sr., a charismatic personality, tightly controls the core philosophy and strategy of the company. From 1995 to 1996, the company closed about 20% of its outlets, as many of them began losing money and the company restructured its operations in Europe. In May 1999, the company announced the appointment of Mr. Jim Pantelidis, an outsider, as the new Chairman and CEO of Bata Ltd.

NIKE, INC.

Nike, based in Beaverton, Oregon, manufactures a wide variety of high quality athletic footwear and other accessories with 1999 revenues of about $9 billion. The company catalog lists over 800 models for use in about 25 different sports and leisure activities. Products are divided into four lines: running, court (basketball and racquet sports), cleated (field sports), and emerging (such as children's shoes and leisure shoes). The company was founded in 1964 by Phil Knight, a long distance runner, who remains Chairman, and his coach, Bill Bowerman, to design lightweight running shoes.

The focus of the company is to create and market its products (shoes and accessories) to males and females between 18 and 34 years. Its success began with manufacturing running shoes for jogging, a popular activity in the U.S. As it expanded, it was faced with the challenge of bringing into its product line shoes popular in other regions (for example, soccer in Europe), resulting in a debate on the extent to which it should market-tailor its products. In each sports line, it tries to target its top-of-the line at the high performance athlete and has several other models for the general user.

The company uses famous sports personalities such as Michael Jordan, Pete Sampras, and Tiger Woods as celebrity spokespersons and "signs" them to lucrative endorsement contracts with the belief that consumers will purchase Nike shoes and remain loyal to a brand name that is so closely identified with successful athletes.

Nike sells its shoes through independent distributors, licensees, and subsidiaries in 110 countries. It monitors its international marketing very closely and is in the process of consolidating distribution centers around the world to serve its coordinated marketing plans. The company's R&D center in New Hampshire seeks new technologies and advanced materials with which to update shoe models at least every six months.

The company, from its inception, has contracted with a variety of manufacturers in Asia to produce the shoes. The focus is on low wage countries that include South Korea, Taiwan, Thailand, Hong Kong, and the Philippines. This spread was also an effort to minimize political risk. As South Korea becomes more expensive, some manufacturing is expected to shift to China. The company has built an extensive system to find and develop contract factories, and closely monitor them for quality. Expatriate technicians work closely with these contract factories. While some of the factories are exclusive, many nonexclusive factories manufacture other shoes too. The company's production system is closely tied to its order booking program wherein retailers often order five to six months in advance of delivery and receive discounted rates.

Production in low cost economies brought Nike some unwanted bad publicity recently for the working conditions in these factories. There is also a risk to operating in varied economies because some countries have experienced volatility in their economic and political environments. Yet, even with changes in exchange rates and tariffs, Nike finds the cost advantage is significant. Apart from the problems related to labor practices in its factories, the late 1990s brought a slowdown in sales and profits. The company is in the process of reinventing itself to reach newer and nontraditional markets with a shrinking of the athletic shoe segment from 38% to 31% of all shoes in the U.S.

1. The company perceives its target consumers as having similar needs across the globe.

    Bata: To a lesser extent   1   2   3   4   5   To a greater extent

    Nike: To a lesser extent   1   2   3   4   5   To a greater extent

2. The firm's definition of the industry encompasses several segments.

    Bata: To a lesser extent   1   2   3   4   5   To a greater extent

    Nike: To a lesser extent   1   2   3   4   5   To a greater extent

3. The parent company is considering diversifying into sporting apparel (swimwear) or fitness equipment. It believes it already has some competence within the company and familiarity with markets to be able to venture into it. This diversification fits with the present strategy followed by the company.

    Bata: To a lesser extent   1   2   3   4   5   To a greater extent

    Nike: To a lesser extent   1   2   3   4   5   To a greater extent

4. If a marketing manager wished to launch a new promotional campaign, he or she would need to obtain prior approval from the parent company.

Bata:	Less likely	1	2	3	4	5	More likely
Nike:	Less likely	1	2	3	4	5	More likely

5. If a production manager wished to change hiring or training practices, he or she would need to obtain prior approval from the parent company.

Bata:	Less likely	1	2	3	4	5	More likely
Nike:	Less likely	1	2	3	4	5	More likely

6. In this company, the production schedule for each plant would need to be closely coordinated with the sales plan on an international basis.

Bata:	To a lesser extent	1	2	3	4	5	To a greater extent
Nike:	To a lesser extent	1	2	3	4	5	To a greater extent

7. This company sees a need for clustering national units into regions for operational efficiencies. What would be the appropriate basis by which to undertake the restructuring?

Bata: Geographic / By product lines

Nike: Geographic / By product lines

8. A subsidiary of this company has identified a new line of footwear for use in schools in their physical education classes. Would prior permission be needed from the parent in order to proceed?

Bata: Prior permission needed / Not needed

Nike: Prior permission needed / Not needed

9. In the light of the responses to the above, what strategy would you say the company is following on an international plane?

   Bata: Global strategy   1   2   3   4   5   Multidomestic strategy

   Nike: Global strategy   1   2   3   4   5   Multidomestic strategy

10. Speculate on trends in the industry over the next ten years with respect to (a) consumer preferences for footwear, (b) national investment policies, and (c) any other. What changes would you recommend the company initiate in its strategy/operations to best face these trends, and why?

    Bata:

    _____

    _____

    _____

    _____

    _____

    _____

    _____

    _____

    _____

_____

_____

_____

Nike:

_____

_____

_____

_____

_____

_____

_____

_____

_____

_____

Strategy Session 12

Understanding Turnaround Management

OBJECTIVE

The purpose of this session is to help develop an understanding of the critical issues surrounding organizational decline and the nature of turnaround management. An understanding of these issues enables managers to better understand the consequences of inaction and assist in developing a viable turnaround strategy. The exercise provides an opportunity to use analytical skills to assess decline and turnaround.

Most management theories are built on the assumption of a firm seeking growth and profitability. Thus, when an organization is undergoing decline in its performance with the prospect of eventual failure, it faces an experience for which it has limited preparation. An understanding of the processes of decline and the principles of effective turnaround management are skills that prospective managers need to have to develop viable turnaround strategies.

Decline in performance is common in the workplace. Most organizations face occasional decline that is quickly reversed. The causes that lead to these drops in performance are external and internal to the organization. External causes include general economic recession, regulatory actions, changes in consumer buying practices, and competitive actions, for example. Internal causes deal with poor management and include a wide range of issues such as over expansion, an improper fit between the company and its environment, poor marketing or product problems, and lack of effective controls. When the managers take timely action in dealing with the causes and reverse the trend, it is a part of the normal

> How few there are who have courage enough to own their faults, or resolution enough to mend them!
>
> —*Benjamin Franklin, Poor Richard's Almanac*

management function. However, research has shown that this does not always happen. In the early stages of decline, managers may deny the severity of the problems, not identify the causes of the problem correctly, and thus the decline continues.

As the firm continues to decline, the severity of the problems worsen and the organization starts incurring cash losses. Other signs may include the exit of valuable personnel. The firm now enters a critical phase and usually it takes some kind of a crisis to shake the organization into realizing the severity of its problems. It could be termination of the CEO, or a bank refusing further credit terms to the organization. When this happens, the firm realizes the need for drastic actions to stem the decline. These actions would be targeted towards cutting costs by improving efficiencies and reducing wasteful expenditures. Employees may be laid off and activities shrunk. The organization may also have to resort to selling assets to raise necessary funds. Quite often at this stage, several members of the top management team may be replaced in order to bring in new skills for the turnaround.

When the decline has been stabilized (that is, when the cash loss has been stemmed), then revenue-generating measures may be instituted such as increasing sales and new product developments. The firm is now on a turnaround path that should be directed towards building its competencies back.

The key principles of turnaround management are precise identification from a strategic perspective of the causes of the organization's decline and turnaround strategies that incorporate key stakeholders.

1. It is important to take care in *identifying the causes of the problems*. Since actions need to be taken to deal with the causes, the more precise the firm is in identifying the problems, the higher the probability of the turnaround effort succeeding. Turnaround management consists of careful review of the causes before actions to correct the problems are defined. Causes of the problems should be grouped into strategic and operational categories. Strategic causes will include: what businesses the firm is in, whether it has the skills to be in those businesses, and how it competes in those businesses. Operational causes will deal with functional areas and include problems in marketing (advertising and promotional issues), human resources (pay, training, etc.), production (plant size, equipment, etc.) and so on.

2. The key point is that *management must deal with the strategic causes*. If the firm does not have the skills to be successful in the business and is experiencing a poor fit with its environment, then it needs to change its direction, reexamine its niche, and perhaps alter the strategy it is following to compete in this business. No amount of operational efficiencies will help if it has not fixed its strategic problems.

3. To achieve a turnaround, the firm needs the *help and support of various stakeholders* such as vendors, distribution channels, customers, bankers, and the like. Part of the skill of implementing the turnaround lies in stakeholder management and the firm's ability to extract concessions from them in the short run. The right leadership is also a crucial factor in successful turnarounds.

Bankruptcy, as an option, is resorted to usually only under extreme circumstances. Under Chapter 7, the firm may opt for liquidation. Under Chapter 11, the firm may seek the protection from creditors while it implements a turnaround plan with the approval of the court. Firms resort to Chapter 11 filing only when they have exhausted all other options and need the protection that the court can give.

 Strategy_Online

Turnaround Management Association is an organization "dedicated to the development of a stronger economy through the restoration of corporate value." To find out about TMA, turnaround management, and its application, visit:

www.turnaround.org

What went wrong with Corel's attempt to take on Microsoft's Office suite with its WordPerfect products is analyzed in this TechWeb online article:

www.techweb.com/wire/finance/story/INV19980223S0005

Exercise: The Decline-Turnaround Sequence

INSTRUCTIONS

Obtain an article from a recent issue of a business magazine or newspaper that describes a company in decline As you read the article, keep in mind the key principles of turnaround management from the reading. Complete the information below individually or in teams.

1.   Define and review the extent of the decline:

_____

_____

_____

_____

_____

_____

_____

_____

_____

_____

_____

_____

_____

_____

_____

_____

_____

_____

2.   What is the crisis? How was the decline recognized?

_____

_____

_____

_____

_____

3.   Changes in the top management team (TMT):

_____

_____

_____

_____

_____

_____

_____

_____

_____

_____

_____

_____

4.   Complete the following table:

Cause of Decline:	Turnaround Actions:
External	Strategic
Internal	Operational

Stakeholders Involved:	Their Role:

5.   Results:

_____

_____

_____

_____

_____

_____

_____

_____

_____

_____

_____

_____

Part III

Implementing Strategy

Strategy Session 13

Succeeding in Strategy Formulation and Implementation

OBJECTIVE

To achieve its objectives, an organization must both formulate and implement its strategies. If either of these tasks is done poorly, the result is the likely failure of the overall strategy. This session provides an understanding of both formulation and implementation.

Early writers in the field of strategic management developed rational planning models that distinguished between strategy formulation and strategy implementation. According to the traditional or rational planning framework, strategy formulation was the role of corporate level managers such as the CEO and other senior executives, and it involved developing a strategy that achieved a fit between the external environment (opportunities and threats) and an organization's internal capabilities and resources (strengths and weaknesses). Once a strategy was formulated or developed, its implementation involved a series of subactivities. These included creating an organizational structure to support the company's chosen strategy and designing performance measurement, compensation, incentives, and controls to achieve the kind of management and employee behavior required for successfully executing the strategy.

I have thought too much to stoop to action.
—*Phillipe Auguste Villiers de L'Isle-Adam*

A revision of the rational planning framework suggests that strategy can emerge in response to unforeseen circumstances. Unplanned responses occur to take advantage of or react to changes in the environment. As a result, the strategies that are implemented look different from what was intended. These effective, but often-unintended strategies, have been labeled *emergent strategies*.

In practice, organizational strategies are probably a combination of the planned and the emergent and often are partially formulated, implemented, and then reformulated to capitalize on strategic opportunities. While it may seem difficult to separate strategy formulation and implementation, since they are closely linked, the two concepts are fundamentally different. In fact, analyzing issues associated with each can provide a useful technique for diagnosing strategic problems.

Framework for Diagnosing Problems   Stated simply, strategy formulation is what you are going to do; strategy implementation is doing it. When an organization chooses to change to a cost leadership strategy (formulation), the execution of that strategy may involve such changes as developing new pricing policies, establishing cost-control procedures, building new facilities, and modifying employee hiring practices and benefits (implementation). If these changes are not carried out successfully, it is impossible to assess the soundness and quality of a given strategy.

The chart in Figure 13.1 shows a way to distinguish between the two concepts in the assessment of strategic performance. The shaded boxes represent the extremes that managers rarely face. In the upper left box, there is outstanding success when the strategy is appropriate and its implementation is sound. All that can be done has been done, and performance indicators are usually strong. The lower right box is exactly the opposite, and performance indicators reveal revenue declines and profit losses. If management tries to improve the strategy, the programs fail because they cannot be executed. If implementation problems are fixed, it results in the execution of a strategy that is not sustainable.

Figure 13.1   Distinguishing Strategy Formulation and Implementation

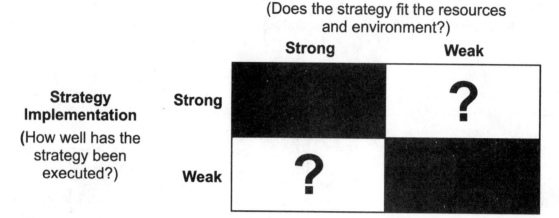

The two question-mark boxes are the ones that practicing managers typically face. The lower left cell involves a situation where the company has chosen a strong strategy that matches organizational resources and capabilities with competitive forces. However, weak implementation will often disguise the appropriateness of the strategy. Because managers are more accustomed to focusing on strategy formulation, the real problem with the strategy (faulty implementation) often is not diagnosed. When performance is low, managers are likely to develop a new strategy rather than question whether the implementation was effective. The new, and perhaps even less appropriate, strategy is then re-implemented and continues to fail.

The upper right box represents situations where an inappropriate strategy is implemented well. The strong execution may overcome the unsound strategy—or at least give management an early warning of impeding problems and the need for a change in strategy. Alternatively, the same strong execution can hasten the failure of the weak strategy. For example, although efficient production and cost cutting measures may bring an organization to a cost leadership position; however, this strategy choice may be inappropriate for the target market.

The important point is that diagnosing problems in an organization requires analysis of strategy implementation as well as strategy formulation. It is critical to incorporate both, since strategic soundness cannot be assessed without reviewing issues involving implementation.

 Strategy_Online

For an executive summary of Procter & Gamble's new direction, go to:

www.pg.com/investors/sectionmain.jhtml

Exercise: Diagnosing Problems at Procter & Gamble

INSTRUCTIONS

Read this short case and then diagnose the problems at Procter & Gamble in the questions that follow.

PROCTER & GAMBLE

Procter & Gamble (P&G), one of the nation's biggest producers of laundry detergents, personal care items (toothpaste, shampoo, bar soap, and the like), foods and beverages, and other packaged goods lines, has struggled with bottom-line problems for a decade. Its profit problems are due to brutal price competition around the world, a stodgy 163-year-old corporate culture that is risk averse, and a stock market that does not favor Old Economy makers of soap. In early 1999, Durk Jager became CEO of P&G, promising a two-year company turnaround.

The Jager formula was to shift the company from its inward cost-cutting focus to one that was outward and emphasized gaining global market share. To achieve this, he stressed new product development, revamping R&D, and cutting the time it took to introduce new products. For example, *Swiffer*, the electrostatic dust mop, was introduced by P&G in 18 months instead of the company's typical three-year development cycle.

Acquisitions were also part of Jager's plan; however, the results were mixed. One success was the purchase and aggressive supermarket distribution of Iams premium dog food, a private brand. Sales reached $1 billion through the mass marketing of this high-margin business. However, Jager ran afoul of investors when he proposed a high-risk acquisition of Warner-Lambert Co. and American Home Products Corp., after having failed in a costly attempt at acquiring Gillette Co.

In his push to make P&G more flexible and responsive, Jager did away with its rigid budget process, which involved lengthy reviews and presentations. Instead, "stretch goals" were instituted where a business segment could spend based on its targeted sales. Jager wanted employees to perform outside their comfort zone and to stop the endless memos and other "Proctoid" behavior that characterized P&G. He changed the old international network of 144 regional managers and reorganized the company into seven global business units around product lines. This gave the company the ability to respond more quickly and efficiently in global trends and was praised by large customers such as Wal-Mart Stores. It was also designed to encourage managers to leave behind the company's traditional consensus management and be more innovative and take more risks.

Unfortunately, the double-digit earnings that Jager predicted by spring of 2000 did not materialize, and the company reported it would fall below target through the third quarter of 2000. From January to June of 2000, the stock price dropped from $118 to $56.

Emails and letters from midlevel managers started to circulate, complaining about morale and a lack of confidence in his leadership. With all of the reorganizations, people complained they did not know who was responsible for what.

Jager resigned after only 17 months in office. P&G is in a retreat phase with new product launches already on the calendar being reconsidered. The new CEO, A. G. Lafley, plans to reverse the trend of changing too much, too fast and is expected to get things done, but in a very positive more traditional P&G way.

1. Describe the strategy developed for Procter & Gamble by Jager. Was it a strong or weak strategy? (To determine if the strategy was strong or weak, review whether it dealt with environmental trends and whether it would offset company weaknesses or capitalize upon company strengths.)

_____

_____

_____

_____

_____

_____

_____

_____

2.   Identify ways the strategy was implemented. Was it executed well? Discuss.

_____

_____

_____

_____

_____

_____

_____

_____

_____

_____

_____

3. In the chart below, place an "X" in the cell that best depicts the Procter & Gamble situation.

Strategy Formulation

	Strong	Weak
Strong		
Weak		

Strategy Implementation

Strategy Session 14

Structuring to Support Strategy

OBJECTIVE

Changes in corporate strategy often require changes in the way an organization is structured. In this strategy session, practice designing new structures and systems for a business as its strategy evolves.

An organization's structure is the formal definition of working relationships between people and departments in an organization. Companies often create organization charts to show who reports to whom and how tasks are divided up. Different structures are required to implement different strategies, and typically structures are changed when they no longer provide the coordination and control necessary to implement strategies successfully.

Management historian Alfred Chandler conducted one of the classic studies dealing with the strategy and organizational structure relationship. After studying U.S. corporations, such as Sears, General Motors, DuPont, and others, Chandler found evidence that when companies changed their strategies, they changed their structures. That is, management set up departments and divisions within the organization to pursue specific strategies, and Chandler labeled this process "structure follows strategy."

Organizational Structures Although there are many structural forms, there are common types in modern organizations. The first is a simple structure where the owner-manager makes all major decisions directly and coordinates all activities. This structure is appropriate for a small, entrepreneurial firm with one or two product lines following a focused cost leadership or a focused differentiation strategy. Employees tend to be generalists.

Form follows function.

—Louis H. Sullivan, founder of the Chicago School of Architecture, in 1896

As companies grow and add several product lines in one industry, the range of tasks that must be performed expands and no one person can successfully perform more than one organizational task without becoming overloaded. The owner-manager, for example, can no longer make and sell the expanded product lines. Employees tend to be specialists in the business functions and are grouped into departments, such as marketing, production, accounting and finance, and human resources, as shown in the simplified organizational chart shown in Figure 14.1. The task of the CEO is to ensure that communication and coordination exists among the departments and that the actions of the departments benefit the entire organization.

Once a corporation diversifies into more than one industry, the multidivisional structure is used. It better equips the organization to handle corporate strategies, which deal with the question of what businesses to be in. As a company expands and diversifies, it becomes more difficult for the CEO to process increasing quantities of strategic information. Therefore, responsibilities for day-to-day operations are delegated to division managers. Employees tend to be functional specialists grouped according to product and market distinctions. How autonomous the divisions are varies from company to company.

Figure 14.1   Functional Structure

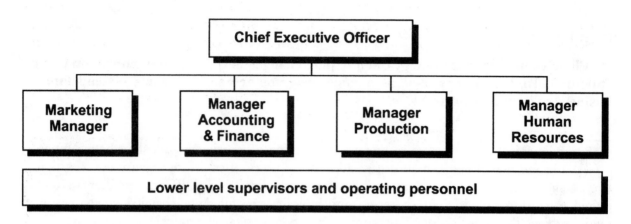

When organizations expand into many areas of business with dozens of different products and markets, the diversity and number of divisions can cause the CEO problems in strategic planning and control as well as overseeing operations. The span of control becomes too large. The solution is to combine several divisions into product groups or strategic business units (SBUs), each under one executive, such as a group vice president. The CEO then can manage the divisions through this level of vice presidents. An example of a Strategic Business Unit organizational chart is shown in Figure 14.2.

Figure 14.2   SBU Structure

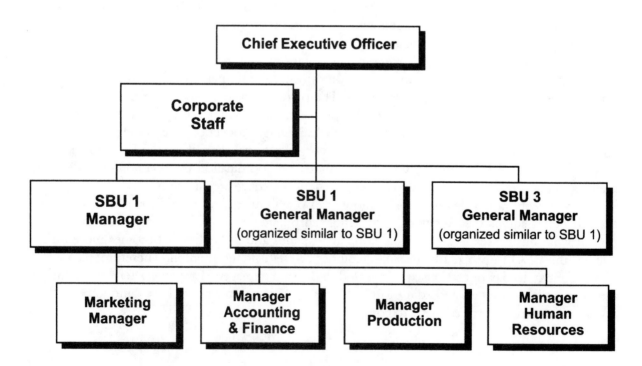

As strategies change, other structures have emerged to serve specific organizational needs. Organizations that manage several projects often use a complex matrix design, which is a hybrid of the functional and the divisional structures. Employees literally work in two departments and have two superiors. For example, an employee in the marketing department reports to the head of marketing but also reports to a product or project manager. Another unique structure is a network-type form, often termed a "nonstructure." The network or virtual organization, as it is also called, is where companies outsource many activities traditionally handled by employees of the organization and thus eliminate in-house business departments.

 Strategy_Online

For articles dealing with this session's topic, visit the online journal Strategy+Business and type the keyword "structure" in the Search box:

www.strategy-business.com/strategy/

Exercise: Designing Organizational Structures for Club Ed

INSTRUCTIONS

Break up into small groups and discuss the strategy and structure for your new resort business as it evolves over the periods described below—and then create an overhead transparency for each period.

TEAM ACTIVITY: PERIOD I

Determined never to shovel snow again, you are establishing a new resort business on a small Caribbean island. The building of the resort is under way, and it is scheduled to open a year from now. You decide it is time to draw up an organizational chart for this new venture, Club Ed. Your initial workforce consists of 15 employees.

a. Develop your generic strategy. Who is the target market? What will be your competitive advantage (cost leadership or differentiator)?

b. What jobs do you need to have covered? What tasks need to be done? What services will you provide?

Work in your group to draw your organization chart and be prepared to discuss your generic strategy and the components and rationale for your company structure.

Your instructor will select one or two groups to present their designs and lead the class discussion.

TEAM ACTIVITY: PERIOD II

You are into your tenth year of operation, Club Ed is wildly successful and you would not recognize a snow shovel if you saw one! You and your partners own 30 Club Eds in a variety of locations in South America, Central America, North America, the Caribbean, and the South Pacific, and the total number of employees is over 400. What are the biggest problems to date? Have you dealt with them in your structure? How have your human resource, control, and information systems developed? Draw an up-to-date organizational chart and prepare to explain your rationale to your classmates.

Your instructor will select one or two groups to present their designs and lead the class discussion.

TEAM ACTIVITY: PERIOD III

Ten more years pass. The Club is now in 50 locations and operates three cruise ships. The fleet of "Love Boats" offers seven-day cruises to the Caribbean, Alaska, and the Far East. Ships include casinos, live music, dancing, nightclubs, and a selection of movies. Food is available around the clock in the main dining rooms. A recent customer profile shows that almost 50% of its customers are repeat business and are 40 years and older. The three "Ss" (sun, sand or snow, and sex) marketing theme no longer appeals to this population in a world where AIDS and fears of skin cancer are all too real. Reservations have been down over the past several seasons as economic conditions fluctuate. How does Club Ed restructure to adapt?

Your instructor will select one or two groups to present their designs and lead the class discussion.

Discussion Questions

1. What is the relationship between strategy and structure?

2. How can Club Ed structure itself as an adaptive organization? Does it always have to react to environmental changes or are there some ways it can be proactive?

Notes

_____

_____

_____

_____

_____

_____

Strategy Session 15

Strategy Implementation Using the 7-S Model

OBJECTIVE

This session will help you recognize the actions that are needed in different areas of the organization to implement strategy and appreciate the interrelationships of these actions. The exercise using the 7-S Model provides the framework for examining them.

A fundamental premise of strategic management is not only should an organization have a good strategy, its organizational members should make it work as well. Implementing strategy involves coordinating a broad range of changes that interrelate. Changing only one or two things seldom brings any significant overall organizational change. To redirect organizations, managers must deal with overlapping and related issues.

The value of a strategy depends not only on the elegance of its conception but fully as much on whether the company proposing the strategy can really execute it.

—Robert H. Waterman Jr.

Strategic management requires a complex interplay of various parts and processes of an organization. If they are all in complete alignment, the organization is successful. A useful way of visualizing these various parts and processes is through the "7-S Model." The model was developed by the McKinsey & Company, the well-known consulting firm, as a framework for thinking about effective management and for bringing about change in an organization. By presenting an integrated view of an organization, it is a useful mechanism to look at the interplay between strategy formulation and implementation. The 7-S framework consists of the following:

1. **Strategy** That set of decisions and actions by which the organization plans to gain competitive advantage by making use of its resources and thereby achieves favorable long-term performance.
2. **Structure** The organization chart, and other means by which an organization divides the tasks to be performed and simultaneously ensures its coordination.
3. **Systems** Procedures (both formal and informal) through which the organization functions on a daily basis. These include budgeting systems, information systems, quality control systems, production scheduling, etc.
4. **Style** The culture, or values and beliefs of the organization, as revealed in the way its members behave.
5. **Staff** The human resources of the organization, recruitment, training, compensation, morale, and so on.
6. **Superordinate goals (or shared values)** Abstract guiding concepts of an organization, shared by most employees, sometimes captured in its mission statement, but may go beyond formally stated objectives.

7. **Skills**   The capabilities of the organization collectively that can be claimed as its competencies.

The basic message of the model is that (a) many factors exist that determine an organization's success; (b) all of them must be in alignment with each other; and (c) they are all equally important. Since all factors are equally important, there is no start or finish to the model.

To use the model, one needs to examine what the current status of each "S" is and then reflect whether changes need to be made to any of the elements for a better fit. It the organization has a strategy that is not working, it could call for a reexamination of the strategy. If an organization's strategy requires innovation and better product development, then the "Staff" should ensure that people with the right skills are being hired and rewarded. The "Systems" should ensure that the monitoring measures track product development. The "Structure" must allow the product development department to access the information it needs and have the authority to make the decisions it needs to make.

Strategy_Online

For an example of how one CEO plans to execute a strategy, read Carly Fiorina—President and Chief Executive Officer of Hewlett-Packard—address to investors:

www.hp.com/financials/textonly/personnel/secanal/0500_sec_fiorina.html

Exercise: Transition at PeopleSoft

INSTRUCTIONS

Read the case in this exercise. Identify data from the case to represent each S in the 7-S Model. Write the information in the relevant box under "Current"—and hand in to your instructor as instructed.

PEOPLESOFT, INC.

PeopleSoft, Inc. is a California-based software company that develops, markets, and supports a coordinated software package to handle accounting, materials management, distribution, manufacturing, supply chain planning and human resources. On an average, a PeopleSoft product costs $1 million. The company grew rapidly, at a rate of 111% between 1990 and 1995. Revenues in 1998 were $1.3 billion, 12 times that of 1994.

Enterprise Resource Planning Industry

PeopleSoft is one of four major players in the $15 billion enterprise resource planning software (ERP) industry. The others include SAP AG of Germany, Oracle Corp., and Baan Co. The ERP industry provides the programs that drive big corporations: financial software for accounting, human resource programs for personnel administration, and manufacturing packages to automate production, with a view to improving efficiencies all around.

The industry saw bad times creep up suddenly. While analysts were forecasting a market of $52 billion in ERP sales by 2002, as the year 2000 approached, firms began focusing on Y2K issues and the market saw sales tapering off. The ERP firms' stock price fell by almost 75%. SAP, the lead player with about one-third market share, saw its stock price fall from $80 in mid-1998 to $23 in a year. Focused on rapid growth, PeopleSoft did not see the slowing of the industry. Revenue from new product sales fell 60% and the stock price that was approaching $60 a share in April 1998 dropped to $11 a year later.

PeopleSoft is the only one of the three big players that relies entirely on enterprise software for its success. While its main customers are midmarket—companies with less than $750 million in annual revenues—Oracle and SAP were trying to enter this same market segment.

PeopleSoft's Origins

David Duffield, formerly a sales executive at International Business Machines, saw an opportunity to develop client-server systems which link individual PCs to a bigger computer serving the whole office. He founded PeopleSoft in 1987 along with a software designer, Ken Morris, and profited from the shift from mainframe computing to networking. PeopleSoft pioneered business management applications able to run on all kinds of systems, and was the first company to do so using Microsoft Windows. The number of employees grew from 914 in 1994 to 7,032 in 1999.

Like most software companies, PeopleSoft built an informal and sensitive corporate culture. David A. Duffield became a legendary, even cult figure within his company. His initials, DAD, suited him appropriately for his role. He routinely schmoozed with workers, and a company rock band was named after him—the Raving Daves. Employees see him as easy-going and not a typical CEO. The company developed its own company lingo where people ate company funded "PeopleSnacks," and shopped at the company "PeopleStore."

The office sometimes has a fun, "theme park" atmosphere. Nerf battles spontaneously break out. There is no dress code. Managers do not have secretaries. Giant posters of smiling employees line the hallways shouting out messages such as "Just try to get me to leave!" Duffield stresses that the company is more than just making money. It is about having fun and having a heart. He has personally given over $200 million to help stray dogs and cats. At 58, Duffield considers himself a family man. He has seven children, of whom four are adopted.

The company has been built on a philosophy that shuns bureaucracy. Executives answer their own phones and write their own letters. Employees are encouraged to say what they think and make important decisions without frequently going to others for help. "Don't ask for permission, ask for forgiveness if something goes wrong" is a company belief. The staff often works 70-hour weeks. PeopleSoft also has an attractive benefits package and employee stock purchase plan. Employees receive a company laptop to use and are free to telecommute from home.

Duffield says the company's main goal is to keep its customers happy. The company spares no expense for that. More than one-third of the company's 1,000 employees are directly involved in customer service. Sometimes, the effort goes beyond the call of duty, such as when a PeopleSoft representative helped a Florida-based company get back in business following Hurricane Andrew. The company had to have its system up and running by the end of the year. The PeopleSoft technician even flew back to Miami on Christmas Day just to make sure things went smoothly.

The company's personnel policies are considered family friendly, too. Fifty-eight percent of new PeopleSoft hires come through an employee referral service program that actively encourages workers to recruit relatives and friends. Duffield's wife, Cheryl, helped found PeopleSoft, and his brother, son and daughter all work there. Dozens of married couples and relatives work within the company ranks. The company has a "Bring your parents to work" day.

Through its rapid growth, Duffield maintained that the key challenge was retaining their corporate culture. He cites the loyalty and enthusiasm of the workforce as something he would not sacrifice in striving for the best possible growth. "Other companies would kill for the kind of commitment we have—and it is primarily due to the culture of the company." However, as the company grew rapidly and the number of employees rose, many newcomers did not feel as much a part of the family as the older employees did. The rapid growth hurt products too. The designers from human resources and designers from manufacturing became focused on their own areas, and the products each group produced did not look alike and work together as well as they should for an integrated management software offering.

There were other internal problems. Bugs in PeopleSoft programs began to increase, and customers started complaining of poor service. "When you're growing at 80 to 90 percent a year, you can make mistakes," Duffield said. "They get covered up." When growth slows, problems begin to surface.

Continued Growth

The acquisitions of other software companies supported PeopleSoft's growth. In 1996, People-Soft acquired Red Pepper Software, a specialist in advanced manufacturing planning, but many thought that PeopleSoft had overpaid for it. Duffield, kept the two organizations separate in order to protect Red Peppers brand identity and also due to his concern about the impact of the acquisition on the company's corporate culture. However, the communication between the two cultures was very poor and at times an outside public relations firm acted as a go-between. In 1997, the company acquired Campus Solutions Inc. as part of its strategy for entering the higher education applications market. In October 1999, it agreed to buy Vantive, a money-losing maker of software used by companies to improve customer service, paying a 60% premium. Analysts felt that PeopleSoft needed to quickly integrate and turn that company around to avoid a negative impact.

In the industry, ERP firms are looking to diversify. SAP has been undertaking major reorganization and is aiming at small clients too. Oracle Corp., the world's second-largest independent software company, also produces the Oracle database and a range of other software tools. Meanwhile, J. D. Edwards, a new company that entered the ERP market in 1997, has captured a significant share of the mid-market.

Asked about persistent rumors that PeopleSoft was for sale. Duffield admits that selling the company looked like a good idea six or seven month ago. However, as PeopleSoft's largest shareholder, he says that is no longer the case. He did confirm that the company was actively seeking a new CEO to lead the company in the new environment.

Name: _____

Directions: Identify each S of 7-S Model using the PeopleSoft paradigm.

Superordinate Goals (Guiding concepts, a set of values and aspirations, often unwritten that may go beyond formally stated objectives. They are succinct, abstract, and mean a lot to insiders.)

Current actions:

Recommendations:

Strategy (Actions planned in response to or in anticipation of changes in the external environment—customers and competition.)

Current actions:

Recommendations:

Structure (The division of tasks and its coordination within the company.)

Current actions:

Recommendations:

Systems (All the procedures, formal and informal, that make the organization work: budgeting systems, training systems, accounting systems, etc.)

Current actions:

Recommendations:

Style (A representation of the organization's culture, it reflects the values and beliefs as demonstrated in symbolic behavior.)

Current actions:

Recommendations:

Staff (The people issues, both hard—pay scales, training programs, etc.— and soft—morale, attitude, motivation, etc.)

Current actions:

Recommendations:

Skills (Crucial attributes of the company, its strengths, and competencies.)

Current actions:

Recommendations:

Strategy Session 16

The Role of Cooperation in Strategic Management

OBJECTIVE

Recognizing the role for cooperation in strategic management and appreciating the individual skills required to cooperate in a competitive economy are analyzed in this strategy session—and in the exercise that follows.

The very term "strategy" evokes a context of rivalry wherein firms are competing with each other in the pursuit of their goals. The business literature is full of aggressive, militaristic metaphors such as "capturing market share" or "making a killing." On the face of it, however, it is difficult to think of cooperation as having a place in strategic management.

However, several theoretical perspectives including agency theory, transaction cost economics, procedural justice, institutional theory, game theory, and resource dependence are now used to study various issues that arise out of cooperation. These include: alliance formation, type of structures, strategy implications, motivation, trust, performance, conflict resolution, and knowledge acquisition or transfer.

Cooperation faces us in the business world in several ways. As you have seen in Strategy Session 10: Global Strategic Alliances, interfirm cooperation in the form of joint ventures, and other forms of alliances (for example, marketing, R&D, and the like) take place almost routinely today, although they are not initially seen as an example of cooperation. The distinguishing feature of these forms is that there is a contract between two parties that spells out the purpose and nature of cooperation and how it will be monitored. When circumscribed by a contract, firms gain more confidence in cooperating, say, fore example, in technology, while simultaneously competing in the market place.

You have to compete and cooperate at the same time.

—Ray Noorda, CEO of Novell Corp.

Nevertheless, cooperation is also required of firms in other areas where there is no contract binding them. They may share information and resources to fight regulation, technological obsolescence, or just aid the general growth of the market.

We need to start with the idea that for one business to do well, it is not necessary for another to fail—which is more often than not the case in the real world. By using game theory, it is possible to conceive of a "value net" that is comprised of competitors, customers, suppliers, and complementors. A competitor can be any player who causes a customer to value your product less, and a complementor can be any player who causes a customer to value your product more. In the personal computer industry, for example, Compaq and Gateway are competitors, but they are complementors to Intel, the maker of computer processor chips, and Microsoft, the maker of computer operating system software. Cooperation between Microsoft and Intel and Compaq benefits technological improvements and overall growth of the market.

The need for competition is built into the free market system we follow. However, increasingly the need is to learn to collaborate in order to compete. This requires organizations to use new measurements of success, different from what was used traditionally, as well as individual managers developing a spirit of trust, commitment, and mutual benefit in order to build links in a spirit of cooperation.

 Strategy_Online

Co-opetition Interactive *is the online complement to the Business Week bestseller Co-opetition, hosted by the authors Adam Brandenburger and Barry Nalebuff. You can find it at this Yale School of Management Web site:*

mayet.som.yale.edu/coopetition/index2.html

Barry K. Allen, Executive VP, Ameritech, discusses cooperation and competition in this online article at the following Illinois Bell Web site:

www.illinoisbell.com/news/release/view/1,1753,3330|381_387,00.html

Exercise: Acting Out the Commons' Dilemma

INSTRUCTIONS

There are two phases in this exercise, which is performed in class. Follow the instructions given for each phase.

PHASE I

Identify situations that require an organization to cooperate with one or more firms in the same industry or in different industries. List the motives for the cooperation in each instance in the table below.

Industry or Names of Companies	Nature of Cooperation	Benefits to Firms from Cooperation

PHASE II

Now, you will have an opportunity to cooperate or compete with your classmates individually. There will be several rounds played and in each, you will have to make a decision to compete or cooperate. You may change your decision from round to round. Decisions will remain anonymous, which means your classmates will not know the decision you have made and only the instructor will know this information. At the end of each round of decision making, the instructor will announce the points earned by a "cooperator" and a "competor" and read some of the reasons provided for the decision.

Each round will proceed as below: Complete the decision slip in Figure 16.1 and describe, briefly in the space provided, the reason for the decision. Submit it for calculation. After the instructor announces scores for "competors" and "cooperators," you will have a few minutes to move around the class to discuss with the others, formulate your strategy, and then make the next decision individually. When scores are announced at the end of each round, keep a running total of your score based on your decision.

POINTS

Each student's goal is to maximize the points that can be scored in the class session over all the rounds. There will be a reward or prize for the students who have received the highest points. The payoff matrix to be used is

Cooperator's score	90% − [(90% / Number students) x Number of competors]
Competor's score	Cooperator's score + 10%

The formula is designed so that one who competes will earn more points than one who cooperates in that particular round. However, if there are no cooperators in a particular round and everybody competes, then nobody gets any points. If everybody cooperates, each individual will earn the same number of points.

DEBRIEFING

After the prescribed rounds are played, there should be 15 minutes of debriefing during which the class explores the motives for decisions and the strategies used.

Figure 16.1   Decision Slip

Name:	Round Number:

Decision: (Check one)

_____ I will compete and take 10 points higher than the cooperators.

_____ I will cooperate and accept 10 points lower that the competors.

Comment: Please briefly explain the reason for your decision.

Strategy Session 17

Social Responsibility of Corporations

OBJECTIVE

Understand the social responsibility of business in an examination of two views.

Social responsibility is the obligation of organizations towards society. The most common approaches to social responsibility reflect either of two very different philosophies. These two views vary in their conception of the level and type of involvement management should undertake in terms of activities to benefit society. In the classical economic approach, business is viewed exclusively as an economic entity whose nearly exclusive purpose is profit. The activist approach, on the other hand, views business as a member of society, with an obligation to set policies and make decisions that will enhance society's welfare.

The Classical Economic Approach   The classical economic approach to social responsibility suggests that a business organization should limit its involvement to activities *that improve its own economic performance.* This approach maintains that the first and foremost responsibility of management is to earn profits for owners (stockholders). According to economist Milton Friedman, a strong proponent of this view, there is a potential conflict of interest when society holds managers responsible to

How to balance the common good and the special purpose of the institution is the question we must answer

—*Peter F. Drucker*

owners for meeting profit goals and at the same time holds them responsible to society to enhance the social welfare. From this perspective, every dollar spent on social problems or donated to a charity is one less dollar distributed to the owners in the form of dividends and one less dollar available for the kind of investment that creates jobs.

Another argument against managers being involved in social responsibility programs is that business lacks the expertise to determine that programs have the greatest needs. For example, should an organization donate to the local YMCA, or is there a program with greater needs?

In sum, the classical approach to social responsibility insists that business organizations have the social responsibility not to do harm to customers, employees, or the environment. However, managers do not have the right to invest stockholders' profits in activities focusing on social problems. According to this view, management's only social responsibility is to follow the legal and ethical rules of society while maximizing profitability.

The Activist Approach   The activist model argues that *business does in fact have a responsibility* to deal with social problems, since business is both part of the cause of these problems and part of society. Moreover, social responsibility activities suggest organizations *do* have the technical, financial, and managerial resources to help solve society's difficult problems. There is evidence that businesses agree with the view. For example, Ben & Jerry's has a PartnerShop program, by which it establishes stores in partnerships with nonprofit organizations that offer job training opportunities to underserved youths and adults. In New York City, the company partnered with Common Ground Community, a group dedicated to ending homelessness. Through this program, Ben & Jerry's waives the standard franchise fees, and the franchise owners/operators retain their business profits to help support their program. Also, Home Depot set up a Team Depot program in 1992 that utilizes the expertise and energy of its employees in community projects ranging from building a playground in Los Angeles' South Central neighborhood to helping residents in Oklahoma City after tornadoes struck the region. In 1999 alone, Team Depot handled over 3,000 projects.

Another part of the activist model argument is that business has a responsibility not just to owners and shareholders, but also to everyone who has a stake in the company's operations. In the activist view, business, as a corporate citizen, has an obligation to respond to the needs of all stakeholders while pursuing a profit. Lastly, the activist argument holds that when business itself takes the initiative in addressing social problems, costly government intervention is less likely.

A Difficult Choice   When law requires an action, or when investment in a socially responsible activity is profitable, no conflict exists between the two views and both approaches would support the activity. When the law neither requires the socially responsible activity nor is the activity in itself profitable, the two approaches differ. The classical view argues against becoming involved; the activist view argues for support of the involvement if the costs are not prohibitively high.

The degree to which a business advances societal versus economic objectives depends to a great extent on factors such as the organization's size, the nature of competition in the industry, the type of problems involved, the costs of pursuing an activity versus the consequences of not doing so, and the personality and preferences of the top management team. Regarding the latter, the founders and current managers of Ben & Jerry's Homemade, Inc., and Newman's Own have strong preferences towards the activist approach. In the case of the ice cream maker Ben & Jerry's, the company makes decisions that are in line with environmental concerns, supplier conditions, and the communities with which it interacts. Newman's Own makes salad dressings, pasta sauces, salsa, and lemonade, and all profits from the company go to charities and social causes.

Part of Strategy Implementation   Both approaches to social responsibility can influence how strategies are implemented. Ben & Jerry's has charged premium prices and gained brand loyalty because of its responsibility to society. In contrast, firms such as Colgate-Palmolive and 3M, which remained in segregated South Africa during the economic sanctions of the 1980s, expanded their base and dominated their South African markets once apartheid ended.

Some criteria that managers can use to make decisions regarding the organization's obligation towards society include:

1. *How the firm views itself, namely its mission.* The mission describes how a company intends to do business and, frequently, its understanding of its social responsibility.
2. *Whether negative publicity will occur and its impact.* Management must view the implications of negative publicity in terms of the company's ability to obtain customers and employees.
3. *What type of additional scrutiny the firm will undergo because of its decisions.* Additional scrutiny arising from regulatory authorities can lead to regulations that are more stringent and restrictions that the company may wish to avoid.

 Strategy_Online

Business Ethics, *an online corporate social responsibility report, is a good resource for this issue:*

www.business-ethics.com

Exercise: Whose Responsibility Is It?

INSTRUCTIONS

Read the situation facing Global Chemical, a fictitious company facing a situation that is a composite of many real-life scenarios. Then answer the questions at the end of this case.

GLOBAL CHEMICAL COMPANY

Several years ago, a citizen environmental group from Kentucky began complaining about the health hazards they claimed were being carried downstream from the processing facility of Global Chemical across the state border in Ashton, West Virginia. Several small towns along the river in Kentucky had been affected by the pollution. They brought in health specialists to support their claims that pollutants from the river were causing serious health problems in these towns.

An independent study conducted by the state of West Virginia concluded that while the residents of these towns did experience higher-than-normal levels of a number of types of cancer, "there is no proven link between these diseases and the chemicals from Global."

Now, despite this lack of proof, it appears that Global Chemical's board of directors will consider the charges against the facility at its next meeting.

As part of the materials to be sent to board members, the CEO would like to include recommendations about what action to take on this problem. The filtering system is too old to be upgraded, and to put in a new system would cost millions and would close the plant for months. Some board members think it would make more sense to build a new plant somewhere else (maybe overseas, where environmental laws are not as strict) rather than put an entirely new filtering system in such an old facility.

Further complicating the situation is the fact that almost half of the workers in this community work at Global. Closing the plant for even a few months not only would cause extreme financial hardship but also would threaten the existence of many local businesses. Understandably, the unions at the company are totally opposed to any actions that might hurt their members, especially since none of the pollution charts have been proven.

The citizens' environmental group from Kentucky is threatening to cooperate with a 60-Minutes-type program that is going to exposé of the situation on national television. If it gets to that point, it might not matter that there is no proof that the chemicals from Global cause the diseases found in the Kentucky towns.

1. Identify Global Chemical's stakeholders in this situation.

_____

_____

_____

_____

_____

_____

_____

_____

_____

_____

_____

_____

_____

2. Whose responsibility is it to deal with the health concerns? Respond according to the following views:

a. Classical economic approach

_____

_____

_____

_____

_____

_____

_____

_____

_____

_____

b. Activist approach

3. What are the company's alternatives?

_____

_____

_____

_____

_____

_____

_____

_____

_____

_____

_____

4. Which alternative would you recommend? Which stakeholders are being satisfied by this decision?

_____

_____

_____

_____

_____

_____

_____

_____

_____

_____

_____

_____

5. What specific steps would you suggest to deal with the other company stakeholder claims?

_____

_____

_____

_____

_____

_____

_____

_____

_____

_____

_____

Part IV

Industry Analysis

Lodging Industry Profile

Information Systems Industry Profile

Template for Industry Analysis

Lodging

As the decade of the 1990s came to a close, the lodging industry had an interesting mix of lower occupancy rates, a drop in construction levels, higher revenues and greater pre-tax profits. Some of the growth problems that led to losses in the early part of the decade were corrected, and aggregate industry profits are expected to grow 8% a year through 2002.

INDUSTRY OVERVIEW

The lodging industry provides accommodations for travelers while they are away from home. On average, business travelers occupy approximately 56% of all lodging rooms. The remaining 44% include vacationers (24%) and people seeking accommodation for other personal or family reasons (20%). The business travelers' needs include basic room essentials, meal services, and communication facilities such as fax machines and in-room Internet access. In addition, meeting rooms, duplicating services, and recreational and entertainment options are frequently desired.

Nonbusiness travelers look for the basic accommodations of bed, bath, telephone, and sometimes meal services. If the location is a destination resort, travelers expect extensive leisure and recreational facilities. The number of nonbusiness travelers has increased over the years due to rising disposable personal income and expanded leisure time. Increases in fuel prices, however, can negatively impact consumer travel behavior. Drivers must pay higher gas prices and airlines must add fuel surcharges, and car rental agencies must increase rates to cover the added fuel costs. Price fluctuations and the state of the economy quickly affect the amount of personal travel, whereas business travel follows turns in the economy by three to six months.

Room rates are higher on weekday nights (Sunday through Thursday) when the business travel is most frequent. However, occupancy levels are higher on weekend nights (Friday and Saturday). The average price per room has increased steadily to $81 in 1999 and is projected to reach $90 by 2002.

For the most part, the lodging industry consists of publicly owned firms such as Cendant Corp., whose brands include Days Inn, Ramada (U.S.) and Super 8. However, some major firms in this industry remain privately held, such as the Radisson Hotels chain, owned by the Carlson Hospitality Group, and the Hyatt Hotels, controlled by the Pritzker family. Mergers and internal growth are causing the industry to become more consolidated, with the most merger activity occurring in 1998. For example, Promus Hotel Corp. merged with Doubletree Corp., and then in 1999 Hilton Hotels acquired Promus. Yet, despite increased consolidation activities, no single lodging chain accounts for more than 10% of the approximate 3.9 million hotel rooms available in the United States.

The lodging industry recorded revenues of $93 billion in 1998 and approximate revenues of $100 billion in 1999. Room sales accounted for 73% of the 1999 revenues, and food sales were 21% of the total. Record pretax profits for 1999 totaled $22.6 billion, compared to $20.9 billion in 1998. The higher revenues and larger profits are due primarily to room rate increases of 4% on average for each occupied room and improved operating efficiency and low interest rates on debt.

---

* This industry profile is required reading for the exercise in Strategy Session 8.

INDUSTRY GROWTH AND OCCUPANCY RATES

The opening of new hotels reached a peak in 1998 because of improved economic conditions and favorable access to capital. The 1,520 new hotels that opened in 1998 were three times the number of start-ups in 1994, the year that the industry began to recover from its slump. This rapid expansion, however, started to slow down in 1999 due to a glut in rooms and a resultant decline in occupancy rates. Occupancy rates dropped from a high of 64.7% in 1994 to a low of 63.4% in 1999.

Typically, overbuilding and a decline in occupancy rates would signal trouble for the industry. Nevertheless, industry profits continue to climb because of a lower break-even occupancy point for the industry. The break-even occupancy level is determined by the initial cost of the property, how that cost was financed, the ability of management to control costs, the actual occupancy rate, and the average price per room. When the break-even occupancy rate drops, it means that fewer rooms need to be occupied before profits are generated. This has resulted in the continuation of an eight-year profit growth record for the lodging industry. Projections, indicated with an asterisk, suggest these trends in occupancy rates and profits will continue through 2001 as shown in Table A.1.

Table A.1 Trends in Occupancy Rates

	1998	1999	2000*	2001*	2002*
Occupancy rate (%)	63.9	63.4	63.0	62.7	62.7
Percentage of rooms sold	3.2	3.5	3.0	2.7	2.7
Average daily rate ($)	78.01	81.07	83.99	87.1	90.4
Break-even occupancy	–	53.6	50.5	–	–
*Projection for indicated year.					

INDUSTRY SEGMENTS

The industry consists of six broad segment types: luxury, first class, midmarket, economy, budget, and extended stay. Into the next decade, positive trends are associated with the high-end and economy properties.

High-end Properties

A trend noted by industry analysts is the preponderance of high-end hotels in development. This can be seen in Table A.2, which lists the number of projects and Table A.3 lists the number of rooms under actual construction and in the permitting stage for each of these segments as of the end of 1999. This data illustrates that a larger number of midmarket and first-class properties have been recently opened and are in the new development pipeline, both in terms of the number of projects and number of rooms.

Table A.2   Hotels in Development—Number of Projects

Segment	Number of Projects				
	Recently Opened	Under Construction	In Permitting	TOTAL	Early Planning
Luxury	9	22	24	46	13
First Class (Upscale)	88	141	133	274	134
Mid-Market (Full Service)	206	167	188	355	165
Mid-Market (Limited Service)	515	385	367	752	341
Economy (Full Service)	33	8	6	14	10
Economy (Limited Service)	189	82	76	158	118
Budget	85	52	132	184	120
Extended-Stay (Upper Tier)	77	83	81	164	123
Extended-Stay (Middle Tier)	88	47	37	84	25
Extended-Stay (Lower Tier)	103	29	17	46	7
Independents	0	3	38	41	88
TOTAL	**1,393**	**1,019**	**1,099**	**2,118**	**1,144**

Note: Based on historical experience, the attrition rate for projects in "In Permitting" can be up to 25% and the attrition rate for projects in Early Planning can be up to 60%. As successful projects move forward, the number of planned rooms frequently decreases. During difficult financing periods, timelines can lengthen, too.

Source: ©Lodging Econometrics, Development Pipeline by category, 4th quarter 1999.

Table A.3   High-end Hotels in Development—Number of Rooms

Segment	Number of Rooms				
	Recently Opened	Under Construction	In Permitting	TOTAL	Early Planning
Luxury	1,929	6,087	6.674	12.761	4,374
First Class (Upscale)	20,797	43,989	45,000	88,989	42,073
Mid-Market (Full-Service)	25,222	21,326	27,864	49,190	25,761
Mid-Market (Limited-Service)	41,887	33,337	32,331	65,668	31,807
Economy (Full-Service)	2,057	539	448	987	630
Economy (Limited-Service)	12,518	5,953	9,750	15,703	9,476
Budget	5,789	3,844	9,499	13,343	8,900
Extended-Stay (Upper Tier)	8,857	8,808	8,330	17,138	12,717
Extended-Stay (Middle Tier)	9,322	5,486	3,663	9,149	2,615
Extended-Stay (Lower Tier)	12,081	3,570	2,022	5,592	839
Independents	0	365	5,942	6,307	16,617
TOTAL	**140,459**	**133,304**	**151,523**	**284,827**	**155,809**

Source: ©Lodging Econometrics, Development Pipeline by category, 4th quarter 1999.

Economy Properties

There is some evidence that an improvement in the occupancy rates of the economy properties will occur in 2000. During the decade of the 1990s, the economy chains were much more affected by the recession in the early part of the decade. They not only did not recover as well as other segments during the mid-1990s, they also faced a steeper decline in occupancy rates in 1999. While occupancy levels in total had dropped to 63.4% for the industry by 1999, the economy segment closed the decade in the 58% range. Overbuilding in this segment during the 1990s resulted in increased supply that was not matched by growth in demand for these rooms.

However, recent patterns in demand signal a possible improvement for this segment. The U.S. coastal markets, specifically San Francisco Bay and South Florida, have very high demand that is matched by the high supply in these areas, giving a strong boost to occupancy rates. In addition, in some markets, such as Ft. Lauderdale, Philadelphia, Austin, Texas, Miami, and Newark, New Jersey, demand growth exceeds the supply of economy properties. These factors suggest that the declining-occupancy cycle for this segment may improve during the next decade.

Industry Concentration

Mergers and internal growth are causing the industry to become more consolidated, with the most merger activity occurring in 1998. The largest U.S.-based hotel company is Cendant Corp., which includes many well-known chains as previously noted. So do the other players in this industry. Table A.4, according to data available as of mid-1999, lists the properties, number of rooms, and the 1998 operating revenues for large hotel companies.

INDUSTRY TRENDS

Trends affecting the lodging industry are diversification by large hotels into other service areas, greater segmentation to spur growth, improved marketing and Internet developments, and the use of labor saving devices.

Service Offerings

Lodging businesses are tailoring their products and services to the customers they wish to attract. For example, hotel companies offer voice mail, fax service, and in-room Internet access that appeal to business travelers. Extended-stay hotels, which provide services aimed at guests seeking a room for a least five nights, feature separate living room areas and kitchen facilities. Cendant Corp. has ownership interests in other service industries, such as real estate brokerage offices and vacation timeshare exchanges. These latter areas offer Cendant the opportunity for cross-promotion and for developing its preferred vendor program. Another hotel company, Marriott International, has moved into the management of retirement communities. Marriott is applying its experience in facilities management and providing hospitality to consumers.

Table A.4 Properties and Number of Rooms for Large Hotel Companies

Company	Major Chains Owned	Number of Properties	Number of Rooms	Operating Revenue (millions)
Cendent Corp.	Days Inn, Ramada (U.S.), Super 8, Howard Johnson, Travelodge (N. America), Knights Inn	6,149	536,703	$5,055.4
Bass Hotels & Resorts	Holiday Inn, Inter-Continental	2,700	450,000	$$1,365
Marriott International	Marriott, Courtyard, Residence Inn, Fairfield Inn, Renaissance, Ramada (outside N. America), Marriott Executive Apartments	1,764	339,200	$7,968
Choice Hotels International	Comfort Inn, Quality Inn, Econo Lodge	4,056	325,326	$165.4
Best Western International	Best Western	3,832	303,943	$161
Accor S.A.	Motel 6, Novotel, Hotel Sofitel	2,762	303,777	$3174
Starwood Hotels & Resorts	Sheraton, Westin	700	223,000	$4,736
Promus Hotel Corp.	Hampton Inns, Doubletree Hotels, Embassy Suites, Homewood Suites	1,362	194,231	$1,107.3
Carlson Hospitality Group	Radisson	570	130,000	na
Hilton Hotels	Hilton (U.S.)	249	87,014	$1,769
	TOTAL	24,144	2,893,194	—

Greater Segmentation

Segmentation involves developing different pricing options, services, and accommodation styles for different types of guests. Companies will continue to use new brands to broaden their customer bases and create value by drawing on resources and skills from one type of facility to another. However, the success of additional segmentation by any one hotel depends largely on whether the sales are being generated from competitors or are cannibalizing a company's existing properties.

The addition of more hotel brands as a means of adding to overall demand for rooms is probably unlikely (given the industry's oversupply of rooms). There is also a potential problem created by the rise in industry brands. An important advantage of being part of a chain is the name recognition it affords. With more brands in the marketplace, there is a tendency for images and brand names to blur together in the consumer's mind.

Marketing and Technology

E-commerce and the use of the Internet to contact properties directly are technological developments that will continue to help smooth sales and the delivery of services. Internet addresses and home pages for hotel chains and for individual properties provide direct access to information about facilities, and travelers are doing their own research about travel choices. In addition, the use of the Internet for booking reservations will continue to grow. An estimated 62% of U.S. hotels use on-line booking of rooms.

Hotel companies are also creating marketing affiliations to boost sales. For example, cross-marketing arrangements with airlines provide consumers with frequent flyer miles for staying at certain hotels.

Laborsaving Devices

The number of employees per 100 occupied rooms has dropped 10% during the past 10 years due to increased worker productivity and laborsaving devices. For example, more automated check-in and checkout services reduces long-term operating costs and boosts customer satisfaction. The automation of various hotel functions is also critical when unemployment levels are low, and it becomes difficult to attract and retain good employees.

INDUSTRY OUTLOOK

The lodging industry is in the mature stage of its life cycle. This is evidenced by the segmentation strategies being developed by key players, the increasing consolidation of the industry, and the trend of hotels becoming members of chains rather than stand-alone properties. Nonetheless, there will always be room for hotels that remain independent, particularly if they have a prime location or distinctive qualities that attract visitors.

Information Systems

Industry Profile

An information system (IS) is a set of interrelated computer components that collect, retrieve, process, store, and distribute information to support decision making, coordination, control, and analysis. The rapid growth of the industry that designs, builds, and markets information systems can be seen in the way the various segments of this industry have emerged within a short period of time and the varied specialization of companies within it. The exponential change in technology in both hardware and software has made this a dynamic landscape, which has transformed several sectors of the economy, especially telecommunications and entertainment. In addition to hardware and software, the IS industry—when broadly defined—includes a thriving peripherals and accessories sector. It also covers services such as maintenance, information technology training, and consulting.

Estimates on industry size vary and can be confusing. As a technology-driven industry, its growth is rapid and new segments emerge all the time. Different definitions of the industry and its segments lead to widely varying estimates of size. For example, one estimate placed the amount spent on all segments of information technology in 1993 at $360 billion and projected that it would grow to $1.7 trillion by 2003. However, another projection estimated that the size of the services component alone would be $1.5 trillion in 2004. The various projections given below are from different experts and must be taken to be broadly indicative.

HARDWARE

The computer hardware industry is broadly classified into three segments: personal computers (including notebooks), systems and servers (including mainframes and supercomputers), and workstations. Hardware accounts for about 40% of the total expenditure on information technology. A common characteristic of the industry is that the price of equipment has fallen as technology has evolved and computing power increased. Consequently, usage has expanded and the market has broadened. In the personal computer segment in particular, new operating systems and powerful processors have resulted in an "upgrade" cycle in which users move up to more powerful computers that optimize both available—and new—technologies.

Traditionally, hardware sales grew largely due to business demand. Yet trends in networking computers and the popularity of the Internet has caused large demands from individual users.

PC Segment

This is the largest segment both in terms of units and dollars. The value of PCs shipped worldwide in 1999 was approximately $190 billion, with the U.S. accounting approximately 40% of this. Desktops made up the bulk of this category at about 80%. Growth was in the range of 20% in the past, but the market slowed down for some time. Recent trends indicate a revival, and the market is now expected to grow at about 15% for the next few years. This segment is also extremely competitive with strong pressures to keep prices low. The industry is responding with falling processor prices and the emergence of "dumb" terminals to connect to the Internet.

The industry also suffers from over capacity. This has necessitated efficient inventory control techniques and put a premium on strategic management in order to maintain profitability. A trend in concentration wherein the top five companies (Compaq, IBM, Dell, Hewlett-Packard, and NEC/Packard Bell) presently hold 45% of the market is expected to continue. The bulk of the PC segment (about 85%) continues to be accounted for by the companies subscribing to the "Wintel" standard (Intel-designed microprocessors using the Microsoft Windows operating system). An alternative standard formulated by Apple Inc. with its Macintosh machines continues to serve only niche markets in education and design. (The Linux operating system is discussed below.)

The Internet poses a mixed challenge to the need for upgrading hardware. On the one hand, advanced graphics requires increasingly sophisticated and faster processors and broadband Internet service (for example, DSL-, cable-, T3-type connections). On the other hand, accessing new and constantly revised Web content does not require new PC hardware.

Systems and Servers

This segment, which includes mainframes, minicomputers, servers, and supercomputers, accounts for about 30% of the industry. Servers have seen a boom in recent times due to the demands of the Internet. Their sales are expected to be approximately $99 billion by 2003. The low-end servers also face competition from powerful desktops with distinctions between categories often blurring. At the low end of this segment, IBM, Compaq, Hewlett-Packard, and Dell are major players. At the high end (mainframes), IBM competes with Fujitsu, Hitachi and NEC.

Workstations

This is the smallest segment of the three accounting for about $15 billion (about 6%) of the industry. These machines combine powerful processors, networking and graphical user interfaces targeted at engineering and scientific applications. UNIX machines that dominated this segment have given way to powerful desktops based on the Windows NT/2000 system. Sun Microsystems and Hewlett Packard are the major players in this market.

SOFTWARE

Software comprises the programs, routines, and symbolic languages that relay instructions from the user to the hardware in order to control its functioning and direct operations. There are two broad categories of software: systems software and applications software.

Systems Software

Systems software manages the computer's resources and organizes the storage of data. Sales of this software are projected to reach a size of $68 billion in 2002. The most common form is the operating system (OS), which varies for different classes of computers (PCs, mainframes, and so on). In the case of PCs, the dominant operating system is Microsoft's Windows system, accounting for about 90% of the market. The Macintosh machines of Apple Computers have their own operating system, the Mac OS. More recently, the Linux operating system software has been attracting a strong following because of the flexibility it offers, running on a variety of machines, and allowing users (the "open-source" community) to customize it—and support a graphical interface that is similar to Windows and Macintosh. Most versions of Linux are free or available for a modest sum. Dell is even selling PCs with a commercial version of Linux preinstalled.

Microsoft's initial agreement with IBM allowed it to freely sell the original DOS operating system. This combined with the open-architecture of the IBM PC quickly led to standardization in the market. Having a standard in operating system allows firms to invest in writing applications software, which really makes the computer useful for general users.

AT&T's Bell laboratories developed the Unix operating system that is popular for workstations. IBM's mainframes run on a system supplied by the company, and VAX minicomputers from Digital Equipment Corporation (now acquired by Compaq) run on the VMS operating system. In the corporate server segment, Windows NT (now called Windows 2000) competes with Novell's Netware.

Other kinds of systems software, apart from operating systems, would include compilers and interpreters that translate programs for the computer to execute and communication software that sends data over a network.

Applications Software

Applications software is the set of instructions that lets the computer perform specific functions, like word processing, spreadsheet accounting applications, and database management systems.. Such software can be written specifically for a particular computer and user, or it can be packaged and sold for general use. An organization may also buy a standard package and have it customized by a vendor or by its own information technology department. Applications software was a $31 billion market in 1998 and is projected to reach $47 billion by 2002.

Some well-known categories of applications software for the personal computer include spreadsheets, word processing, databases, presentation graphics, and drawing applications. Some of these are packaged into "office" suites and the leader in this segment of the industry is Microsoft Office, followed by Lotus SmartSuite from IBM and WordPerfect Office from Corel. PC utilities help enhance the computer's operations and Symantec is a leader here followed by programs from Network Associates and Computer Associates. A category of products that combines education and entertainment is also very popular. It is a market that is about $8 billion and growing at about 22%. The leaders in this segment include CUC International, the Learning Company (acquired Broderbund Software), and Electronic Arts. These compete with game systems from Sony and Nintendo, which also use dedicated software supplied by these same firms. With a rash of virus attacks paralyzing many systems, the market for virus software has grown considerably benefiting firms like Network Associates, which markets McAfee VirusScan, and Symantec, which markets Norton AntiVirus.

Application software for mainframes is often supplied by the mainframe manufacturers themselves, namely IBM, Fujitsu, Hitachi, and NEC. In addition, independent vendors such as Computer Associates have become major players. The vendors target product categories such as data center management, peripherals management, data security, maintenance tools, and accounting tools. Database management systems (DBMS) have been growing at about 15% and companies like Oracle, Sybase, Computer Associates, and Informix are leaders in this market. The rising computing power of PCs has led to networking of PCs that behave like mainframe computers. Companies like Microsoft, Novell, and Banyan Systems are meeting the resultant need for network operating systems.

Enterprise Resource Planning (ERP) is the term given to a category of software products that automates back-office business processes to help manage an organization's everyday activities. This segment saw rapid growth for several years before slowing down to a market size of about $17 billion in 1999 although it is expected to grow to $66 billion by 2003. Major players in this market include SAP (Germany), PeopleSoft, and Oracle. This market has since slowed down. A related set of products that helps improve the front office (also called *customer relationship management software*) includes automating sales, call centers, and the like, and is expected to rapidly grow to approximately $16 billion by 2003.

Web Browsers

This software helps end-users access the World Wide Web, and it is typically distributed "free" or bundled with other software. Currently, Microsoft's Internet Explorer dominates with a 75% market share. The other major browser, Netscape's Navigator, which is part of a suite of Internet-related applications sold as Netscape Communicator, has about 23%.

COMPUTER PERIPHERALS

This segment deals with the manufacture and distribution of products considered accessories such as storage devices, printers, monitors, scanners, CD-ROM burners, and so on. The increasing use of computers in many sectors of the economy apart from the rapid growth of the World Wide Web has resulted in a rapid growth in demand for data storage capacity, being met by companies such as EMC Corp., Sun Microsystems, IBM, and Storage Technology.

GENERAL

The IS industry constantly faces a different set of competitive dynamics driven by the changing nature of technology and the discovery of new applications for it. The oft-quoted Moore's law (after Intel cofounder Gordon Moore) states that computing power doubles every 18 months. The absence of clear standards, typical of emerging industries, adds to the complexity. Within hardware, mainframes and PCs are considered by some to be relatively mature. In software, systems software is considered more mature where a few established players compete for market share. In this situation, success depends on an installed base, powerful distribution channels, and effective sales organizations. Often, the cost and time to switch makes customers stay with the same product.

Application software is a vast area that offers several attractive niches to encourage market entry. The success of firms in this segment will depend on not only the originality and creativity of their product but also their ability to utilize distribution channels to reach the customer in a cost efficient manner.

A result of changing technology is that product life cycles have become shorter and less predictable, especially in the case of application software that rests on system software that is constantly undergoing revisions and upgrading.

The services sector within the IS industry has benefited in many ways and the commercial services part (as different from the consumer services) is estimated at $99 billion in 2004. Rather than invest in hardware and software, many firms outsource their IS needs. A new group called *application service providers* (ASPs) lease out expensive software for firms to use—or alternatively offer a comprehensive service to run the systems for a firm. Companies such as EDS, Computer Sciences Corp., and IBM Global Services seek to take over completely the IS functions of the company or at least tap into an estimated 50% of a firm's IS budget spent on maintenance and related functions.

The regulatory environment for the IS industry is going through a period of discovery. Three areas of flux exist:

1. The extent to which innovations in software can be patented is an unclear area that attracts lawsuits and has limited case law on which to draw.
2. The need for security of information, privacy or transaction, and vulnerability of equipment from virus attacks will see increasing regulation.
3. E-commerce is presently exempt from sales tax and as the volume of business transacted continues to grow exponentially, the likelihood of this status continuing is not known. In addition, the antitrust trial of Microsoft has also raised several issues related to how rules of market behavior in traditional industries can be applied to the new high technology sectors.

The global nature of this industry reveals itself in many ways. For one, many of the segments discussed are at different stages of development in different countries. Furthermore, the technology commands a global market, and virtually all of the companies mentioned here operate as global companies. The rapid growth of the IS industry has widened the gap between demand and supply of professionals in the western countries. Salaries have risen faster in this sector, and immigration into the United States has not eased the crunch. Just as in the manufacturing of mature products, many firms have found it easier to export operations to low-cost economies, such as India, have become very competitive as centers for development of software. The technology has also allowed labor-intensive operations such as transcribing text, operation of call centers, and so on to move overseas where wage scales and other costs are lower.

Template

for Industry Survey

An industry survey provides important information to understand why firms follow the strategies they do. It also provides management with needed data in formulating competitive strategies. This template will help you gather the information in a systematic manner to create an industry profile. Once all of the information is gathered, it provides the framework for further analysis of industry trends and competitive strategies.

INDUSTRY OVERVIEW

1. **Identification/Definition of the industry**
   Brief description of the products or services produced by competitors in the industry, major players, SIC code.

2. **Origin of industry**
   Historical description including events that affected its profitability, major inventions/innovations that affected the industry.

3. **Location of industry**
   Initial location of the industry, whether geographical clusters exist, importance of being close to markets or inputs.

PLAYERS IN THE INDUSTRY

1. **Size of firms in the industry**
   Sales, capacity and asset base of firms, existence of a minimum efficient size of plant, trends in concentration.

2. **Organizational structures**
   Nature of organizational forms in the industry, private vs. public ownership.

3. **Industry restructuring**
   Trends in restructuring of firms in the industry, tendency to diversify, backward/forward integrate, and reasons for the same.

4. **Interfirm arrangements**
   Extent of cooperation within the industry, alliances, joint-R&D projects, activities of the trade association, lobbying efforts and relations with the government.

5. **Substitute industry(ies)**
   Are there substitute products or services from another industry that appear to be different but can satisfy the same need (for example, bottled water a substitute for cola, fax a substitute for shipping via U.P.S., and wine a substitute for beer)?

OTHER INDUSTRY CHARACTERISTICS

1. **Value creation methods and costs**
   Description of production/value creation process, inventory standards.

2. **Inputs/Suppliers**
   Availability of suppliers, supplier concentration trends, nature of competition in the input or supplier industries, price trends, level of technology and important trends.

3. **Markets**
   Volume of sales in units and value in the industry, distribution channels, selling methods, consumer profile, nature of use of the products of the industry, trends in consumption. What are the products and services that meet the basic need?

4. **Human resources**
   Extent of unionization in the industry, union-management relations, availability of different classes of personnel, training practices.

5. **R&D and Innovation**
   Nature of R&D in the industry, its importance, distribution of patents, rate of innovation and productivity.

6. **Finance**
   Sources of financing in the industry, difficulty in attracting capital.

FUTURE INDUSTRY TRENDS

Limits on future growth of the industry, domestic and international competition, regulation.

SOURCES OF INFORMATION

COMPUSTAT
Forbes Magazine (mid-January issue)
Industry Norms and Key Business Ratios (by SIC codes) (HF5681.R25 I52)
Ivestext (CD-ROM/Information Access Co., Belmont, CA)
Manufacturing USA: Industry Analyses, Statistics, and Leading Companies (HD4907.M662)
Moody's Investors Fact Sheets: Industry Review (HG4907.M662)
Predicasts F&S Index Europe (HF1040.9.E8P72)
Predicasts F&S Index U.S. (HF1040.8.P74)
Predicasts F&S Induex International (HF54.U5P7)
Specific Industry Trade Publications (e.g., *Beverage Industry, Computerworld, American Banker*)
Standard & Poors, Industry Surveys (HG4902.S82)
Standard Industrial Classification Manual, Washington, D. C. (PrEx 2.6/2: In 27/987)
Value Line Investment Survey (HG4501.V26)
Ward's Business Directory of U.S. Private and Public Companies (HG4057.A458)

Part V

Semester Projects

Team Projects A & B

MICA Method Of Case Analysis and Discussion

T e a m   P r o j e c t s

Project A: Comparing Two Organizations in the Same Industry

Project B: Identifying Strategic Issues at Local Business Organizations

OBJECTIVES

These guidelines for two team projects help prepare you and your team for studying strategic issues that organizations face in the context of their environment.

A basic model of strategic management stipulates that there be a fit between the firm and its environment in order for the firm to achieve its long-term goals. Both of the projects described below provide a framework for analyzing the strategy of a firm in relation to its environment. Teams that work on Project A will compare and contrast the strategic issues faced by two competitors in the same industry. If access to a local organization is possible, Project B is another option that gives teams an opportunity to analyze the strategic management process and its various components at a nearby firm.

Teams should comprise four to six learners. Each project is divided into phases as described in the left column of their respective table. . In the right column, relevant Strategy Sessions or Industry Profiles have been suggested for the teams to review that provide examples of how to apply analytical models to company situations.

PROJECT A: COMPARING TWO ORGANIZATIONS IN THE SAME INDUSTRY

Phase I Industry Analysis	Strategy Sessions / Industry Profiles
1. Choose an industry.	See Part IV – Industry Profiles and the Template for Industry Survey
2. Gather information on the industry.	
3. Analyze the industry. What can you conclude about the attractiveness of the industry over the next three years?	Strategy Session 6 - Factors of Competition Model.
Phase II Two Competitors in Industry	
Identify two companies that are operating in the industry you have studied. Preferably, choose two that have had very different performances in the recent past. Divide the team into two subunits, and each unit will focus on one firm.	

Phase II Two Competitors in Industry (cont.)	Strategy Sessions
1. Each team subunit should identify the current strategy of the firm and appraise its internal resources and capabilities. How is the current strategy incorporating these competencies and helping the firm compete within the industry?	Strategy Session 7 Generating a plan of action—SWOT Analysis Strategy Session 8 Developing Generic Strategy Strategy Session 9 Viewing Corporate Strategy from the Core Competencies Perspective Session 15 Strategy Implementation Using the 7-S Model
2. Evaluate the current performance of the firm. How successful has the strategy been in generating an above-average financial performance of the firm over time and in relation to the industry and competitors?	

Phase III Final Analysis	
Reunite both subunits of the team and conduct the final analysis.	
1. Compare the two firms. Faced with the same industry environment, examine how and why the firms pursued the strategies they did.	
2. What are your recommendations for each of them? How would you change their strategies? What recommendations do you have for implementation?	

PROJECT B: IDENTIFYING STRATEGIC ISSUES AT LOCAL BUSINESS ORGANIZATIONS

Phase I   Company Selection
Identify an organization in your local community. This must be a firm that you have access to, both physically in terms of being able to visit the offices and plants, and in being able to meet with and interview at least one company official. The company may be small or large and could operate in either the for-profit or nonprofit sector. If it is a large organization with divisions in several industries, such as Philip Morris, choose one of the divisions for this study.

Phase II Overview	Strategy Sessions / Industry Profiles
Identify the industry in which the organization (or division) competes.	See Part IV Industry Profiles and the Template for Industry Survey
1. Gather information on the industry.	
Analyze the industry. What can you conclude about the attractiveness of the industry over the next three years?	Strategy Session 6 Factors of Competition Model

Phase III Strategic Issues Identification	Strategy Sessions
1. Identify one or two major strategic issues the company faces. To develop a summary of the issues, do either of the following:	████████████████████
a. Develop a table of the definitions of strategy applied to the company. Analyze results from an intended versus emerged strategy perspective, which the definitions help to clarify.	Strategy Session 2 Understanding the Concept of Strategy
b. Examine the current status of each of the parts and processes of strategy. The strategic issues are the elements that do not fit.	████████████████████
2. After undertaking your analysis based on publicly available information, meet with company officials and discuss your findings. Use their input to further refine your analysis.	Strategy Session 15 Strategy Implementation Using the 7s Model

REPORT FORMAT

Present your project work in the form of a written report and an oral presentation to the class. In the case of Project B, you may consider giving a copy of your report to the organization, or inviting the company official who was your contact to the class presentation. Your written report should:

1. Be no more than about 6,000 words (12 pages). Place all tables and charts in appendixes in the end.
2. Organize the report to follow the phases of the project.
3. Include a complete list of references at the end of all published information, web sites, and interviews that were sources of information.

Your presentation should be about 20 minutes. Do not repeat of all the information in the report, but plan your presentation around the key points you wish to convey to the audience.

MICA

Method of Case Analysis and Discussion

The analysis of case studies is one of the most popular techniques for applying strategic management theory to real-life situations. Typically, you read a factual account of a problem or issue faced by an organization and then come to class prepared to discuss the situation and make recommendations.

The MICA method is an approach to case discussion that is designed to increase student preparation and bring about full-class participation. Its focus is on discussion of the case versus a formal presentation of the case by a team of students. There are four main components to the MICA process:

1. Students submit before class a proposed strategic-level and an operational-level action step (a recommended course of action that the company should take).
2. During the class, a student team administers the case discussion.
3. Class members discuss the action steps proposed by the class and vote on the most acceptable course of action.
4. The instructor evaluates the students based on what they say at the time they say it using established MICA scoring criteria.

For each case that is assigned, a team of students administers the case discussion. The remaining students submit action steps to this administrative team before the entire class meets to discuss the case.

ACTION STEPS

Action steps are suggestions to improve the situation described in the case. Each student submits one proposed course of action that is strategic in nature and another that is operational or functional in scope (see Strategy Session 1). For example, a strategic action step might be to sell off one of the company's divisions or to change the company's generic strategy from differentiation to cost leadership. An operational or functional action step might be to develop a new advertising campaign or hire more people in the accounts payable department. The action steps do not include any justification for the proposed action; the students provide justification later during the class discussion.

ADMINISTRATIVE TEAM

The administrative team collects action steps, compiles them, types a listing, and distributes them to the class either just before or during class. The action steps are grouped into two main categories: strategic and operational. The author's last name is shown at the end of each action step in parentheses. Because it is common for two or more students to submit similar action steps, there may be multiple authors for an action step. The team may list authors in the order in which the steps are received, determine the order of authors according to the completeness of the action step submitted, or list authors on a random basis.

The administrative team does not present or discuss the case but rather is responsible for *administering* class discussion. The team's roles include a chairperson, a counter, and as many recorders as needed. In small classes, teams may consist of as few as two persons (chairperson-recorder roles being combined and a counter) to as many as six (three students handle compiling and typing the action steps; the other three students conduct the case discussion as chairperson, counter and recorder).

The counter keeps track of how many times each class member has been called on and assists the chairperson in selecting speakers. This process is designed to provide an equal discussion opportunity for those who wish to participate. The recorder puts on the board any action steps that were modified at the start of class. He or she lists all action steps being discussed and records the outcome of each action step.

PROCESS

1. Introduction

The administrative team arrives early to class. Action steps are distributed to the other members of the class as they arrive. The team signals the start of class by introducing all members of the team, identifying the company to be discussed, and the time frame on which the discussion should center.

2. Modifications of Action Steps

To begin the case discussion, the chairperson asks if the team has compiled any modifications or amendments to the action steps. For example, a member of the class might suggest that Step 5, which is to sell the clothing division of the company, is similar to Step 12, which is to divest an operation. The administrative team consults with the authors of both steps and decides whether the steps should be combined.

3. Discussion of Strategic-level Step

Once the proposed action steps have been modified or clarified, the team begins discussion of strategic-level action steps by selecting the first action step from the list. Those from the class who authored the action step are called on first to provide their rationale for the proposed course of action. (Because the authors of a particular action step are called on first, they have the opportunity to present the strongest arguments, which is the basis for the scoring system.) Once the authors have completed their discussion, any class member who wishes to support or argue against the step raises his or her hand and is called on by the team chairperson. The administrative team is responsible for cutting off "long-winded" discussions and terminating discussions of a particular course of action when arguments become redundant.

After an action step has been thoroughly discussed, the administrative team conducts a vote of the class whether to accept or reject the action step. If accepted, it becomes a fact of the case. At this point, the administrative team randomly chooses three or four strategic-level action steps (usually from an envelope containing the numbers for each action step). Then the class votes on what step to discuss next. Class members may vote for more than one step; and the chairperson breaks any ties. This process continues until all strategic steps are discussed or until the administrative team feels it is time to move on to operational-level steps.

4. Operational-level Action Steps

The administrative team guides the discussion of operational-level courses of action in the same way that the strategic steps were handled. This continues until approximately 10 to 15 minutes before the class period ends. Typically, the majority of strategic-level action steps are discussed and three or four operational-level steps are covered.

5. Closing the Case Discussion

The administrative team ends the discussion of action steps 10 to 15 minutes before the class period ends. (Typically, there are operational-level action steps that are not discussed. However, students are reminded that the major emphasis of the course is on strategic decision making.) Then the chairperson asks the class if anyone prepared research that was not used during the class discussion ("unspent research"). One article per class member is allowed, and students receive additional credit based on their oral summary of the article's content as it applies to a particular action step. These summaries are brief and take 1 to 2 minutes at most.

The administrative team delivers a brief summary of the decisions made by the class and asks its members to spend a few minutes thinking about their class discussion. Have they helped the company with their strategic decisions? Did they notice any pattern in the steps chosen or in the class's discussion? For example, during one session, every action step got a "no" vote. Several class members noted this was because the company had been losing money, and people were reluctant to make any major changes.

SCORING

The instructor, seated at the back of the room, assigns points to class members based on the content and frequency of their arguments. Each time a student speaks, he or she may earn from 0 to 4 points plus bonus points judged by the instructor. Authors of action steps speak first and have the greatest opportunity to back up their argument with facts not yet given. This means, of course, that authors tend to accumulate points quickly. In addition, the first time any class member speaks, he or she is awarded one bonus point regardless of content to encourage participation and give evidence of attendance.

For each case, a student may earn a minimum of 0 and a maximum of 25 points. Students receive points only if their comment is relevant to the action step being discussed, if it contains a supportive argument, and if it is not a repeat of what was said by another student earlier in the discussion. The score for each member of the administrative team equals the highest points allocated to any student for that day; thus the team has an incentive to keep the discussion moving along so that fellow class members will score points.

When the last action step has been discussed and the vote recorded, the instructor asks if any class member feels that he or she was discriminated against (for example, consistently had hand up but was not called on). If a student indicates that this occurred, the instructor asks the administrative team's counter (a) how many times the class member was called on in a nonauthor priority call; and (b) excluding author calls, what was the average number of times students were called on that day. The administrative team comments on the alleged discrimination; and the instructor considers his or her own observations, the statements of the student and the administrative team's statements. If it is judged that discrimination occurred, the student is given one to three first discussion opportunities (after the authors) during the next case. In addition, 3 to 10 pints may be deducted from the case grade of each member of the administrative team for that case. Under these circumstances, bona fide cases of discrimination rarely occur.

Scores are posted on a spreadsheet at the end of class, using student identification numbers for confidentiality.

INSTRUCTOR'S ROLES

The instructor's roles are coaching, scoring, altering the course of debate during the case discussion as required, enforcing MICA rules as needed, and providing a wrap-up at the end of the period. The instructor may intervene at any time during the class for the purpose of guiding discussion or coaching students.

For example, the instructor may accept or reject an action step without allowing discussion if it is deemed a standard business practice or it is too trivial to be discussed given the context of the case. Suppose the class voted to discussion an action step such as "The company needs a mission statement." The instructor should stop the process, remind the class that this action step as it stands is a normally expected business practice, and it would be difficult to develop arguments against this step. The author should develop a proposed mission statement and submit it as an action step, which can then be debated.

Coaching is a way of showing students how to score points. It is used extensively in the first few cases or in a trial case. An example of coaching would be an intervention by the instructor after a student comment. The instructor would note that the student did not score points because someone else had already made the comment or that no points were scored because the research presented did not apply to the action step being discussed.

If necessary, altering the course of debate is important, particularly during the early cases. If the class discussion moves away from the specifics of the action step being discussed and if the administrative team does not quickly refocus the discussion, the instructor must interrupt immediately and note what has happened, reminding the class that no points are awarded for these digressions.

At the end of the period, the instructor asks the class members if, in their opinion, they have helped the company. Students comment on their perceptions, and as the semester progresses, they usually become more aware of the quality of their decisions. For example, one group discussed a company that had been a takeover target and had high levels of debt. Yet in the wrap-up session, the group noted that, although they considered the debt when discussing courses of action (difficult to get loans for expansion and the like), the final strategies they recommended did not help the company become more solvent. Several students noted that the class lost sight of the company's difficult debt situation and relied entirely on management's bright forecast for future sales and earnings.

The instructor can also use the end-of-session comments for a review of the case, updated the case information, or highlight important issues that the students did not cover in their action steps. A few minutes highlighting the key points of the discussion gives students a sense of satisfaction that they hit the important issues or an insight on how a key learning of the case got missed in the discussion.

SUMMARY

Student preparation for class discussion of cases is extensive. Since points are awarded based on information to support or rebut an action step, students read the cases very thoroughly. For example, it is not atypical for students to cite phrases from the case text, as well as information from tables and footnotes. Discussion is also lively. Since points are based primarily on how often students speak and what they say, class participation is very strong.

In addition, some preliminary evidence suggests that students using the MICA method reported better preparation and participation benefits as compared to students using other methods of case discussion. Also, students using the MICA method were better able to identify the main focus of the cases discussed, showing a better recall of content issues involved in case discussions.

References and Sources

STRATEGY SESSION 1

L. J Bourgeois III, I. M., Duhaime, and J. L. Stimpert. 1999. *Strategic Management: A Managerial Perspective*, 2nd ed., pp. 10–11. Forth Worth, TX: The Dryden Press; Michael E. Porter. 1996. What is strategy? *Harvard Business Review* 74(6): 61–78; Brent Schlender. 2000. The customer is the decision maker: Jerry Yang talks with *Fortune's* Brent Schlender about flexibility, hierarchy, and the "religion" of Yahoo. Fortune.com. <http://www.fortune.com/fortune/2000/03/06/ pro5.html.>

STRATEGY SESSION 2

Charles W. L. Hill and Gareth R. Jones. 1998. *Strategic Management: An Integrated Approach*, 4th ed., p. 3. Boston: Houghton Mifflin. Michael A Hitt, R. Duane Ireland, and Robert E. Hoskisson. 1999. *Strategic Management: Competitiveness and Globalization Concepts and Cases*, 3ed., p. 5. Cincinnati: South-Western College Publishing; Charles W. Hofer and Dan Schendel. 1978. *Strategy Formulation: Analytical Concepts*, p. 4. St. Paul, MN: West Publishing; Henry Mintzberg. 1987. Five Ps for strategy. *California Management Review* 30(1): 11-25.

STRATEGY SESSION 3

Dereck E. Abell 1980. *Defining the Business: The Starting Point of Strategic Planning*. Englewood Cliffs, NJ: Prentice Hall; James C. Collins and Jerry I. Porras. 1996. Building your company's vision. *Harvard Business Review* 74(5): 65–77; Jim Collins. 1997. It's not what you make, it's what you stand for. *Inc.* 19(14): 42–45; Jerry Knapp. 1992. A mission statement. *Firehouse*, March: 70–71; Lance Leuthesser and Chiranjeev Kohli. 1997. Corporate identity: The role of mission statements. *Business Horizons* 40(3): 59–66.

STRATEGY SESSION 4

Sources for Part I of the Exercise: R. L. Simison. 1994. GM board adopts formal guidelines on stronger control over management. *Wall Street Journal*, March 28: A4. *Note:* The authors are grateful to GM for providing the full set of guidelines. The guidelines were first adopted in January 1994 and revised in March 1999. An abridged version is provided for this exercise.

Sources for Part II of the Exercise: Business Wire Inc. 1998. Michael Eisner introduces board of directors. *Business Wire Inc.*, February: 24; Bruce Orwall. 1997. If a company prospers, should its directors behave by the book? *Wall Street Journal*, February 24: A1.

STRATEGY SESSION 5

R. E. Freeman. 1984. *Strategic Management: A Stakeholder Approach*, pp. 25, 53–54. Boston: Pitman; Charles W. L. Hill and T. M. Jones. 1992. Stakeholder-agency theory. *Journal of Management Studies* 29: 131–154.

The Exercise was adapted from "A Stakeholder Approach to Strategic Management: An Experiential Learning Exercise," developed by Dr. D. Jeffrey Lenn and published in the 1991 *Proceedings of the 28th Annual Meeting of the Eastern Academy of Management,* 135–137. Used with permission.

Sources for the "U. S. versus Microsoft Corporation": Time. 1999. Microsoft enjoys monopoly power. November 15: 60–65; *The Economist.* 1999. Microsoft and the future. November 13, 1999: 21–23; *The New York Times.* 1999. U.S. judge declares Microsoft a monopoly stifling a market; Gates dissents, favoring talks. November 6: A1, B4–B5; John R. Wilke. 2000. For antitrust judge, trust, or lack of it, really was the issue. June 8: A1, A8; *The Wall Street Journal.* 2000. Judge orders Microsoft broken in two, imposes tough restrictions on practices. June 8: A3, A12.

STRATEGY SESSION 6

Michael E. Porter. 1979. How competitive forces shape strategy. *Harvard Business Review* 57(2): 137–145; Thomas L. Wheelen and J. David Hunger. 2000. *Strategic Management and Business Policy,* 7th ed., pp. 60–61. Upper Saddle River, NJ: Prentice Hall.

STRATEGY SESSION 7

Kenneth R. Andrews. 1980. *The Concept of Corporate Strategy.* Homewood, IL: Richard D. Irwin; Fred R. David, 1999. *Strategic Management Concepts,* 7th ed., pp. 180–184. Upper Saddle River, NJ: Prentice Hall: H. Weihrich. 1982. The TOWS Matrix: A tool for situational analysis. *Long Range Planning* 15(2): 54–66; Robert A. Pitts and David Lei. 2000. *Strategic Management: Building and Sustaining Competitive Advantage,* 2nd ed., pp. 10–11 Cincinnati, OH: South-Western College Publishing.

Source for "Robin Hood": Copyright © 1991 by Joseph Lampel, University of Nottingham, England. Reprinted with permission.

STRATEGY SESSION 8

Michael E. Porter. 1985. *Competitive Advantage.* New York: The Free Press; Michael E. Porter. 1991. Towards a dynamic theory of strategy. *Strategic Management Journal* 12: 95–117. James F. Lincoln. 1961. *A New Approach to Industrial Economics,* pp. 126–127. New York: The Devin-Adair Company.

Source for Exercise and Team Activity: Adapted from Anisya Thomas. 1999. Introducing students to business policy and strategy: Two exercises to increase participation and interest. *Journal of Management Education* 23(4): 428–437. Used with permission.

STRATEGY SESSION 9

J. B. Barney. 1991. Firm resources and sustained competitive advantage. *Journal of Management* 17: 99–120; J. B. Barney. 1995. Looking inside for competitive advantage. *Academy of Management Executive* 9(4): 56; R. M. Grant. 1991. The resource-based theory of competitive advantage: Implications for strategy formulation. *California Management Review* 33: 114-135; G. Hamel and C. K. Prahalad. 1994. *Competing for the Future*, p. 227. Cambridge, MA: Harvard Business School Press.

Sources for "Walt Disney Company": Business Week. 2000. Millionaire buys Disney time. June 26: 141, 144; Bruce Orwall. 2000. Michael Eisner's new agenda: Details, details. *Wall Street Journal.* January 26: B1, B4; Bruce Orwall and Matthew Rose. 2000. Disney may sell *Los Angeles Magazine* as it pares down noncore operations. *Wall Street Journal.* January 19: B7; Paul P. Harasimowicz Jr., Martin J. Nicholson, John F. Talbot, John J. Tarpey, and Thomas L. Wheelen. 1996. The Walt Disney Company, Capital Cities/ABC merger (revised). In *Strategic Management and Business Policy*, 7th ed., Thomas L. Wheelen and J. David Hunger, eds., pp. 12-1–12-30. Upper Saddle River, NJ: Prentice Hall; Anthony Claro, Michelle Hill, Eric Maxwell, Russell Porter, and Angela West. 2001. Walt Disney Co. In *Strategic Management Competitiveness and Globalization, 4th ed.*, Michael A. Hitt, R. Duane Ireland, and Robert E. Hoskisson, eds., pp. C-639–C-652. Cincinnati: South-Western College Publishing; Walt Disney Co. *Annual Report.* 1999.

STRATEGY SESSION 10

P. A. Sudarsanam. 1995. *The Essence of Mergers and Acquisitions.* London: Prentice Hall; M. Y. Yoshino and U. S. Rangan. 1995. *Strategic Alliances.* Boston: Harvard Business School Press.

Sources for "NUMMI: The General Motors-Toyota Alliance": Donald W. Nauss. 1999. GM, Toyota team up to develop technologies, *Los Angeles Times.* April 20: C1; Lindsay Chappell. 1998. Chief of Toyota pickup plant got his schooling at GM. *The San Diego Union-Tribune.* September 19: C4. Michael Macoby. 1997. Farewell to the factory: Auto workers in the late twentieth century. *Harvard Business Review* 75(6): 161–168; Harvard Business School. 1991. New United Motor Manufacturing, Inc. Case #9-189-125; Clair Brown and Michael Reich. 1989. When does union-management cooperation work?: A look at NUMMI and GM-Van Nuys. *California Management Review* 31(4): 26–44.

STRATEGY SESSION 11

Christopher A. Bartlett and Sumantra Ghoshal. 1989. *Managing Across Borders: The Transnational Solution.* Boston: Harvard Business School Press.

Sources for "Bata Shoe Organization" profile: Bata Limited. 2000. About us. Bata.com. <http://www.bata.com/main.html>; J. D. Daniels and L. H. Radebaugh, eds. 1998. Bata Ltd. In *International Business*, 130–133. Reading, MA: Addison-Wesley; Betty J. Punnett. Bata Shoe Organization. In *Experiencing International Business and Management*, 2nd ed., pp. 127–128. Belmont, CA: Wadsworth Publishing Company; Bernard Simon. 1996. Bata in transition. *The Financial Times Limited.* June 6: 28.

Sources for "Nike, Inc." profile: Nike, Inc. 2000. Ask Nike. Nike.com. <http://www.nike.com>; Austin, M. Jill. 1997. Nike, Inc.—1996. In *Cases in Strategic Management*, Fred R. David, ed., pp. 495–511. Upper Saddle River, NJ: Prentice Hall; Harvard Business School. 1998. Nike (A)

(Condensed). Case #9-391-238; Lee, Louise. 2000. Can Nike still do it? *Business Week*, February 21: 120–128.

STRATEGY SESSION 12

C. Gopinath. 1991. Turnaround: Recognizing decline and initiating intervention. *Long Range Planning*, 24(6): 96–101; Charles. W. Hofer. 1980. Turnaround strategies. *Journal of Business Strategy* 1: 19–31; D. K. Robbins and John A. Pearce. 1992. Turnaround: retrenchment and recovery. *Strategic Management Journal* 13: 287–309.

STRATEGY SESSION 13

Kenneth R. Andrews. 1971. *The Concept of Corporate Strategy*. Homewood, IL: Dow Jones Irwin; Henry Mintzberg. 1978. Patterns in strategy formulation. *Management Science* 24: 934–948; R. A. Burgelman and A. S. Grove. 1996. Strategic dissonance. *California Management Review* 38(2): 8–28; Thomas V. Bonoma. 1985. *The Marketing Edge: Making Strategies Work*. New York: The Free Press: 10–14; Cornelis A. DeKluyver. 2000. *Strategic Thinking: An Executive Perspective*. Upper Saddle River, NJ: Prentice Hall: 56–57.

Sources for Exercise: Matt Murray and Emily Nelson. 2000. New P&G chief is tough, praised for people skills. *Wall Street Journal*, June 9: B1; Emily Nelson and Nikhil Deogun. 2000. Course correction: Reformer Jager was too much for P&G. So what will work?—Under new boss Lafley, firm still has a need to get its sales growth moving—another earnings warning. *Wall Street Journal*, June 9: A1; Ellen Neuborne and Robert Berner. 2000. Warm and fuzzy won't save Proctor & Gamble. *Business Week*, June 26: 48–50.

STRATEGY SESSION 14

Alfred D. Chandler. 1962. *Strategy and Structure*. Cambridge, MA: MIT Press; Joseph A. Litterer. 1980. *Organizations: Structure and Behavior, 3rd ed.* New York: John Wiley & Sons; J. R. Galbraith and R. K. Kazanjian. 1986. *Strategy Implementation: The Role of Structure and Process, 2nd ed.* St. Paul, MN: West Publishing Co.

Source for Exercise: Adapted from Cheryl Harvey and Kim Morouney. 1998. Organizational structure and design: The Club Ed exercise. *Journal of Management Education* 22(3): 425–430. Used with permission.

STRATEGY SESSION 15

R. H. Waterman, Thomas J. Peters, and J. R. Phillips. 1980. Structure is not an organization. *Business Horizons*, June: 14–26; Dexter Dunphy and Doug Stace. 1993. The strategic management of corporate change. *Human Relations* 46: 905–920.

Source for PeopleSoft case: George Avalos. 1999. Pleasanton, Calif.-based software firm workers welcome new president. *Contra Costa Times*, May 25; David Einstein. 1998. Lean look works at PeopleSoft. *The San Francisco Chronicle*, August 7; D1 Jessica Guynn. 1998. Pleasanton, Calif.-

based PeopleSoft invites workers' parents for a day. *Contra Costa Times*, August 7; Jessica Guynn. 1999. Executive describes pain at California-based PeopleSoft after layoffs. *Contra Costa Times*, January 30; Quentin Hardy. 1999. A software star sees its "family" culture turn dysfunctional, *Wall Street Journal*, May 5: A1; Bryce G. Hoffman. 1999. Calif.-based PeopleSoft reclaims place as software leader, *Contra Costa Times*, September 19; *Business Wire, Inc.* 1999. Peoplesoft names Craig A. Conway as chief executive officer. September 21.

STRATEGY SESSION 16

Adam M. Brandenburgher and Barry J. Nalebuff. 1996. *Co-opetition.* New York: Currency Doubleday; Joel Bleeke and David Ernst. 1998. Collaborating to compete. In *The Strategy Process,* 3rd ed., Henry Mintzberg and James Brian Quinn, eds., pp. 362–366. Upper Saddle River, NJ: Prentice Hall.

Source for Exercise: Adapted from Gary M. Throop. 1989. All managers have a commons (sic) problem: Instruction effects vs. payoff structure in a commons dilemma simulation. Paper presented at the 1989 Eastern Academy of Management Annual Meeting, Portland, Maine. Used with permission.

STRATEGY SESSION 17

Milton Friedman. 1970. The social responsibility of business is to increase its profits. *New York Times Magazine*, September 13: 33, 122–126; Neil Jacoby. 1973. *Corporate Power and Social Responsibility*, p. 6. New York: Macmillan; Frederick D. Sturdivant and Heidi Vernon-Wortzel. 1990. *Business and Society: A Managerial Approach,* 4th ed. Homewood, IL: Irwin.

PART IV

Sources for "Lodging Industry" profile: American Hotel & Motel Association. 1999. Directory of Hotel & Motel Companies (provides addresses, phone numbers, executives' names, property and room totals, and other information). Ahma.com. <http://www.ahma.com>; American Hotel & Motel Association. 1999. Lodgingmagazine.com. <http://www.lodgingmagazine.com>; Grant Flowers. 1999. U. S. Lodging Industry to Report Record Profit of $22.6 B for '99. *Travel Weekly* 58(102): 1–2; Thomas Goetz. 1998. Lodging industry starts to scale back on rapid growth. *Wall Street Journal*. September 29: B4; Lodging Econometrics. 1999. *Fourth Quarter 1999 Report;* Lodging Hospitality. 2000. Lodging growth continues to slow. *Lodging Hospitality* 56: 20; Mark V. Lomanno. 2000. Occupancy-rate projections optimistic for economy properties. *Hotel & Motel Management* 10: 42.; Mike Malley. 2000. Industry performance shows signs of rebound. *Hotel & Motel Management* 215(2): 3–4 ; PriceWaterhouseCoopers. 1999. Lodging Research Network. Lodgingresearch.com. <http://www. lodgingresearch.com>; Smith Travel Research. 1999. *Lodging Outlook and Monthly Newsletter* (data on the U.S. lodging industry). STR-Online.com. <http://www.str-online.com>; Standard & Poors. 1999. *Industry Surveys.* September 2.; U.S. Department of Commerce. 1997. Economic Census: Accommodation and Foodservices, North American Classification System—sector 721. Census.gov. <http://www.census.gov/econguide>.

Sources for "Information Systems Industry" profile: Standard & Poor's Industry Surveys. 2000. *Computers: Commercial Services* 168(22): 1–31, *Computers: Consumer Services and the Internet* 168(11): 1–34, *Computers: Hardware* 168(24): 1–35, and *Computers: Software* 168(9): 1–37; Business Week. 2000. Personal computers: Are the glory days over? February 14: 50; Steven Alter. 1999. *Information Systems: A management perspective.* Addison-Wesley, Reading MA.

PART V

Sources for "MICA Method of Case Discussion": Ramarao Desiraju and C. Gopinath. In press. Encouraging participation in case discussions: A comparison of the MICA and the Harvard case methods. *Journal of Management Education;* Julie Siciliano and Gordon M. McAleer. 1997. Increasing student participation in case discussions: Using the MICA method in strategic management courses. *Journal of Management Education* 21(2): 209–220.

Index